Douglas Liversidge is a journalist and author of many years experience who has written a number of biographies and books on historical subjects, as well as exploration stories. They include *Crown and People*, *Parliament*, *The House of Lords* and *The Luddites*. He has also written three other highly successful royal biographies: *Queen Elizabeth II: The British Monarchy Today*, *Prince Philip: First Gentleman of the Realm* and *The Queen Mother*. His latest bestselling book, *The Mountbattens: From Battenberg to Windsor*, describes the vivid history of this notable dynasty and its long association with the British Royal Family.

Also by Douglas Liversidge

Crown and People
Parliament
The House of Lords
The Luddites
Queen Elizabeth II: The British Monarchy Today
Prince Philip: First Gentleman of the Realm
The Queen Mother
The Mountbattens: From Battenberg to Windsor

Douglas Liversidge

Prince Charles

Monarch in the Making

PANTHER
GRANADA PUBLISHING
London Toronto Sydney New York

Published by Granada Publishing Limited
in Panther Books 1979

ISBN 0 586 04670 4

First published in Great Britain by
Arthur Barker Ltd 1975
Copyright © Douglas Liversidge 1975

Granada Publishing Limited
Frogmore, St Albans, Herts AL2 2NF
and
3 Upper James Street, London W1R 4BP
1221 Avenue of the Americas, New York, NY 10020, USA
117 York Street, Sydney, NSW 2000, Australia
100 Skyway Avenue, Rexdale, Ontario, M9W 3A6, Canada
PO Box 84165, Greenside, 2034 Johannesburg, South Africa
CML Centre, Queen & Wyndham, Auckland 1, New Zealand

Made and printed in Great Britain by
Richard Clay (The Chaucer Press) Ltd
Bungay, Suffolk
Set in Linotype Pilgrim

Contents

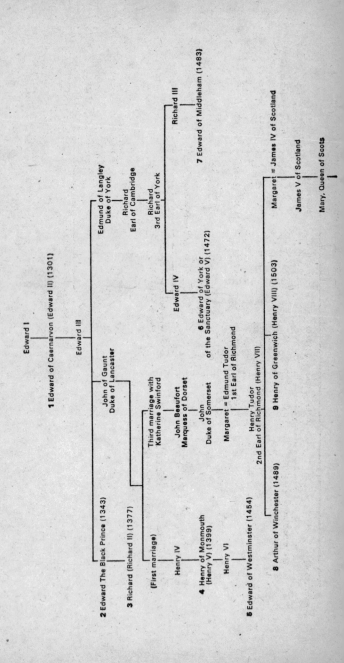

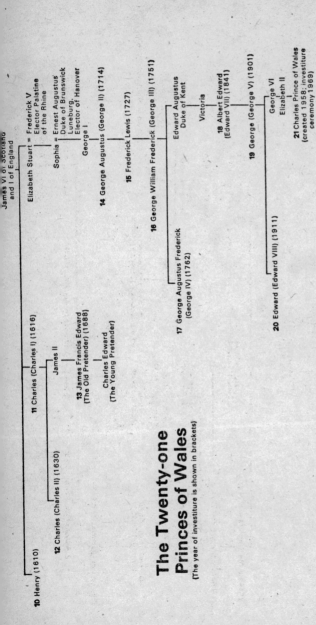

The Twenty-one Princes of Wales

(The year of investiture is shown in brackets)

James VI of Scotland
and I of England

10 Henry (1610)

11 Charles (Charles I) (1616)

Elizabeth Stuart = Frederick V
Elector Palatine
of the Rhine

12 Charles (Charles II) (1630)

James II

Sophia = Ernest Augustus
Duke of Brunswick
Luneburg,
Elector of Hanover

George I

13 James Francis Edward
(The Old Pretender) (1688)

Charles Edward
(The Young Pretender)

14 George Augustus (George II) (1714)

15 Frederick Lewis (1727)

16 George William Frederick (George III) (1751)

Edward Augustus
Duke of Kent

Victoria

17 George Augustus Frederick
(George IV) (1762)

18 Albert Edward
(Edward VII) (1841)

19 George (George V) (1901)

George VI

Elizabeth II

20 Edward (Edward VIII) (1911)

21 Charles Prince of Wales
(created 1958; investiture
ceremony 1969)

1 Blueprint for a Royal Future

On the ninth of November in the year 1841, at Buckingham Palace, Queen Victoria characteristically made this entry in her journal: 'At 12 minutes to 11 a fine large boy was born. O, how happy and how grateful do I feel to that Almighty Providence who has really blessed me so peculiarly.' She might have further enlightened that, some hours earlier, adhering to an archaic custom that a minister of state should attend a royal birth, Sir James Graham, on seeing the infant in the midwife's arms, had remarked: 'I congratulate your Majesty most warmly; a very fine boy, if I may say so.' 'A very fine *prince*, Sir James,' corrected the indignant queen from the curtained four-poster bed. It was a lofty status that neither the future King Edward VII nor his intimates were ever permitted to ignore.

How strikingly different it was when, 107 years later almost to the day, an heir was born to Victoria's great-great-granddaughter. To Queen Elizabeth II, in spite of his exalted station, Prince Charles has always been primarily a son. Not that the Queen is less alert than her forebears to the dignity and prestige of monarchy; indeed today the royal fabric is dyed as deeply in purple as it ever was, but the starch has been allowed to wear away.

Apart from any external factors, a self-imposed metamorphosis in the court itself is quite blatant. Even the strict formality within the royal family alone – sometimes accompanied by an excess of discipline – has gone. The well-known remark by King George V, for instance – 'my father was frightened of his father; I was frightened of my father; and I'm damned well going to see to it that my children are frightened of me' – may have been tinged with a degree of exaggeration. Yet there was much of the martinet in this sailor-king, although fundamentally, beneath the gruff façade, there was also kindness.

'We were, in fact, figuratively speaking [wrote his eldest son, the Duke of Windsor], always on parade, a fact that he would never allow us to forget. If we appeared before him with our Navy lanyards a fraction of an inch out of place, or with our dirks or our sporrans awry, there would be an outburst worthy of the quarter-deck of a warship. Another greeted the appearance of one of us – it may well have been me – with hands stuffed into trouser pockets. Lala (the nanny) was immediately summoned and ordered to sew up the pockets of all our sailor suits, a royal command which, despite some inward reservations, she did not dare to disobey.'

Prince Albert, the second son, at times a victim of verbal chastisement, later reacted to such stern paternal discipline, ensuring as Duke of York and subsequently as King George VI that his children would be spared that treatment. As sovereign, however, he still required his grandchildren to bow and curtsey, a royal ritual that was finally abolished on his daughter's accession. Times had indeed changed. In Victoria's day the air of formality had been so keen that the Prince Consort had insisted that ladies-in-waiting should rise to open the door for the heir apparent. Yet in contrast Prince Philip, noticing a servant hurry to close a door that Prince Charles had failed to close, commanded: 'Leave it alone, man. He's got hands. He can go back and do it himself.'

The character of the court changed with the demise of King Edward VII, when its light-hearted cosmopolitan atmosphere vanished with him. Although the royal residences did not revert to Victorian austerity, the court scene was now essentially British and more staid. Unlike his egregious, pleasure-loving father, King George V was extremely conservative, virtually shunning social life. He and Queen Mary symbolized quiet domesticity, invariably dining alone together, or with relatives, unless they were obliged to entertain in their official role. The Duke of Windsor revealed that they 'seldom accepted invitations to private dinners, and then only to a few "great houses" '.

Before the convulsions of the First World War one thing went unaltered: inexorable rules of custom were not challenged, prevailing both at Buckingham Palace and in the exclusive sphere in which monarchy was traditionally pre-eminent. When the sovereign resided in London, for instance, no officer of the Brigade of Guards would ever dine without wearing white tie and tails, or top hat and frock-coat or morning-coat when in the streets. This and much more was swept away in the deluge of international strife. Indeed two world wars were the funeral pyres not only of long-standing customs but of most of the royal dynasties in Europe.

Changes are wrought by time and by circumstance. It is not that the specific functions of royalty have changed in the twentieth century, but, as the Duke of Windsor once stressed, 'the atmosphere surrounding the British monarchy has completely changed. People are more outspoken, and nobody escapes criticism any more ... There is nothing surprising in the fact that amidst all the changes that have taken place, after two world wars ... the institution of monarchy is no longer a sealed house in a storm.'

In the golden years of empire and invincible world power, Edward VII could proudly proclaim: 'By profession I am a king.' It was enough for monarchy merely to exist, accepted – regardless of their foibles or the way they conducted their lives – as the unshakeable apex of British society. But three years after the Second World War, when Prince Charles was born, there must have been some who queried whether he would ever succeed to the throne. They were chaotic, unstable times. War had broken down many class barriers and the social revolution that had begun in the reign of George V had by now gathered in tempo. Unpredictable in its outcome, it was clear that Britain was entering a new phase in her long history. A Labour government was in power, foisting on the nation its programme for nationalized industry. By controlling 'the means of production, distribution and exchange', socialists visualized a Britain in which economic and political power, snatched from the rich, would be vested in the nation. To some this Marxian philosophy, spawning, it claimed, a classless society, seemed a sinister augury for the monarchy.

Yet on that cheerless and chilly night of 14 November 1948, signs were singularly lacking that the royal family might cease to be enshrined in the people's hearts. Acting on their uncanny instinct for history, thousands of London's loyal citizens gathered in a seething mass outside Buckingham Palace, patiently awaiting any morsel of news. That dreary Sunday night was the culmination of months of expectancy, since the brief announcement on the eve of Derby Day that 'Her Royal Highness The Princess Elizabeth, Duchess of Edinburgh, will undertake no public engagements after the end of June'.

The news had released a torrent of gifts – among them a ton and a half of nappies from the United States – so that a room in the Palace had to be allocated for distributing layettes to other expectant mothers. For the still-unborn royal child the Linen and Woollen Drapers' Institution, of which the Princess was patron, engaged twenty-five retired dressmakers in their cottage homes to produce a layette of fifty-five garments. At the Palace itself the schoolroom, now adapted into a nursery, had returned to the role it had held in the Princess's own childhood. From a storeroom came the cot that had served Elizabeth and others since Victoria's reign; it was now refurbished, not in blue or pink but in yellow silk, so that 'no one can guess whether we want a boy or girl,' the Princess confided.

Nature would decide. The Buhl Room, not long ago the setting for the sombre operation for vascular obstruction affecting the King's legs, was now arranged for the Princess's happier *accouchement*. Already in the Palace post office the official telegrams had been prepared, awaiting dispatch abroad to the King's governors-general and ambassadors; only the word 'Prince' or 'Princess' remained to be inserted. Yet not until it was turned ten o'clock at night would this be done. From the Privy Purse door a blue-liveried footman walked across the dark courtyard to the expectant crowd. 'It's a prince,' bawled a police inspector, and to the rest of the world the tape-machines clattered out their message: 'The Princess Elizabeth, Duchess of Edinburgh, was safely delivered of a Prince at 9.14 p.m. today. Her Royal Highness and her son are both doing well.' Only the people in the Soviet Union and the Communist satellites went in ignorance of the Prince's birth.

For the first time in sixty-two years a child had been born in Buckingham Palace. The last had been the niece of King Edward VII, the daughter of his third brother Arthur, Duke of Connaught. But, though comparisons are odious, the latest birth had greater significance: unless fate intervened, the royal infant was the first to be born certain of kingship since the birth of Prince Edward – later Edward VIII – at the White Lodge in Richmond Park fifty-four years earlier. This future monarch, who, to his mother's delight, weighed 7 pounds 6 ounces at birth, was the fifth in descent from Queen Victoria and eleventh from the Electress Sophia of Hanover (the granddaughter of the Stuart James I), whose heirs-general, according to an eighteenth-century parliamentary decree, succeed to the British throne, assuming they accept the Protestant faith.

But the little boy's ancestry was much more complex and unique. As Mr Dermot Morrah, Arundel Herald Extraordinary, once wrote, the child was also

'... 13th from James I (of England) and VI (of Scotland), who united the two Crowns of Great Britain, 32nd from William the Conqueror, tracing through the senior Yorkist line, though he was also descended from John of Gaunt, the ancestor of the Lancastrian kings; and 39th from Alfred the Great (from which point the Anglo-Saxon chronicles carry the pedigree back in direct male line to the God Woden). He was 14th in descent from Mary, Queen of Scots; 23rd, through her, from Robert the Bruce (or 22nd through the Bowes-Lyons, the family name of the Queen Mother); and 28th from St Margaret. Through Henry Tudor he was 24th in descent from Llewellyn-ap-Gruffyd, Prince of All Wales. Through his father, the Duke of Edinburgh, he had the blood of Harold II, last of the Anglo-Saxon kings, and was the first male-line descendant of the kings of Denmark in the British royal family since the death of King Harthacnut in 1042. In the remoter regions of the pedigree may be found many of the great names of history and romance : Charlemagne and St. Louis and Frederick the Wonder of the World; Vortigern and Cadwaladr; Neill of the Nine Hostages and the High Kings of Erin; even Musa ibn Naseir, an Arab sheikh who was born in Mecca in 660. But one only has to look back six generations – one more than to Queen Victoria though along a different line – to come upon such modest names as George Smith and Mary Browne.'

But it was the future rather than the past that concerned most people. Indeed from the time when the fountains in London's Trafalgar Square gushed blue at his birth, no childhood career this century has inspired more idle talk and conjecture – and, furthermore, such controversy. It has been claimed that Prince Charles was launched on the public scene with the expertise applied in promoting a commercial product. Nothing could be more remote from the truth. Although we live in times of ephemeral sport and 'pop' stars, screen and television idols, all synthetic heroes and heroines clamouring for the headlines and cheap popularity, happily in this highly commercialized and materialistic age the members of the royal family stand aloof from its artificialities and make-believe; whereas many public figures today pander to that American creation, the image machine, the British royal family commendably shun the bogus and remain their natural selves.

The Queen, for instance, presents no false image; indeed, there is no attempt to conceal the fact that if she has a penchant at all, or dedication outside her constitutional duties, it is for bloodstock and such events as the Badminton Trials. And irrespective of public re-action, Prince Philip makes no attempt to conceal his enthusiasm for technology, for the polo field on Sundays, for deer-stalking, game-shooting and the sea.

The folly of creating a false image – certainly in royalty – was noticeable in Prince Charles's attempt to be seen in the likeness of his father. The mannerisms and the stance, even the mode of speech, were painstakingly copied with almost embarrassing results, especially as he tends more to the reflective qualities of the Queen rather than to the extrovert attitude of Prince Philip. Fortunately his own traits – some of which were already pronounced in childhood – have been allowed to emerge, leaving a personality impressive in its own right.

Now in young manhood, speaking about his image and the people who want him to change it, he says: 'I was asked in Australia whether I concentrated on developing or improving my image – as if I was some kind of washing powder, presumably with a special blue whitener. I dare say that I could improve it in some circles by growing my hair to a more fashionable length, being seen in the Playboy Club at frequent intervals and squeezing myself into excruciatingly tight clothes ... I have absolutely no idea what my image is and therefore I intend to go on being myself to the best of my ability.'

There is, however, an element of truth in the suggestion that Prince Charles has so far spent his life in a unique experiment in which he is being groomed for kingship in an egalitarian age. It is an unarguable fact that over the centuries the monarchy, whether voluntarily or by coercion, has kept in step with the current mood. But as Prince Charles once said in a radio interview: 'In these times this sort of organization [the monarchy] is called into question – it is not taken for granted as it used to be. In that sense one has to be far more professional than I think one ever used to be.' Today much of the success or failure of the British monarchy depends greatly on the personality and attributes of the one who wears the crown. To that extent Charles's education and training generally – the most liberal given to an heir apparent in the centuries-old story of the British throne – was especially designed with that in mind.

On reflection it now seems that the experiment began the night Prince Charles was born. For many years it had been the custom for a minister of the state to verify a royal birth, a procedure harking back to the day in July 1688 when the consort of the Roman Catholic James II delivered a son. Furious at the thought of a Catholic succession, the Protestant Whigs foolishly denounced the new-born infant as a changeling, smuggled into the Queen's bedchamber in a warming-pan. The charge was utterly false, merely illustrating the degrading machinations to which politicians will at times resort.

But it started a long tradition whereby someone responsible to Parliament was present at a birth to ensure the legitimate claim if he ascends the throne.

Although home secretaries had witnessed the births of his two daughters, George VI now thought it was time to probe the validity of the practice, finally discovering that it was neither a constitutional necessity nor backed by parliamentary decree. He therefore consulted the government and, through his private secretary, announced that it was 'merely the survival of an archaic custom, and the King feels it unnecessary to continue further a practice for which there is no legal requirement'.

And so Mr James Chuter Ede, the Home Secretary in Clement Attlee's Labour Government, merely waited by his telephone to receive news of Prince Charles's birth.

The second surprise in the Prince's infancy was the announcement a month after his birth that he would be known as Prince Charles. His full names were Charles Philip Arthur George, the second and fourth being those of his father and grandfather. The third – conjuring up the undying romance of the Arthurian legend – was, if anything, the most noble known to British royalty. But the name Charles seemed to have been abandoned for ever with the death of the second Charles in 1685. When, therefore, Princess Elizabeth and Prince Philip christened their second child Anne almost two years later, it was widely believed to be a deliberate reversion to the names of the royal Stuarts. One could be excused for reflecting on the ill-fated romance of Bonnie Prince Charles, but in fact the choice of 'Charles' and 'Anne' was due solely to the fact that they were the names most favoured by the children's parents.

During the morning of 15 December 1948 Charles's names were officially registered at Buckingham Palace by Mr Stanley Clare, the registrar at Caxton Hall in the City of Westminster, and in the afternoon the infant Prince was christened by the Archbishop of Canterbury, aided by the Dean of the Chapel Royal. A Nazi aerial attack had destroyed the Palace chapel in September 1940, so the ceremony was held in the white-and-gold Music Room. From Windsor came the Lily Font that, designed by Prince Albert, had been fashioned for the baptism of Queen Victoria's first child in 1840. Into it was poured water contained in a Hebron phial from the River Jordan, a practice that originated with the Crusades. The infant's robe of Honiton lace and satin was equally ancient, having been worn by all Victoria's children and many other royal offspring since then. Prince Charles bore his christening with the same resignation as he was to demonstrate at other times in later years, and thus entered the Protestant Church of England, a paramount requisite for reaching the throne. Like any other British child of that time, he also received a ration card and state-decreed libations of orange juice.

Prince Charles was in his eighth month when his parents moved to a new home – Clarence House, a huge square mansion not far from Buckingham Palace. Once the residence of the Duke of Clarence (who succeeded to the throne as William iv), it had been derelict and unoccupied for some thirty years, apart from serving as a temporary wartime home for the British Red Cross.

Clarence House, where another Duchess of Edinburgh, the Russian princess who married Victoria's second son, had also resided, was antiquated even by Victorian standards. The unsightly network of plumbing was extremely out of date and inadequate, and so were the bathrooms, while wartime utilitarian electric fittings had been installed because the gas lighting was effete. But gradually, out of the dust and rubble, emerged an exquisite home, with a neighbouring house in Ambassador's Court serving as domestic and secretarial offices.

Close to York House (for a while the home of the last Prince of Wales), Clarence House faces The Mall and St James's Park. On the top storey, overlooking the park and garden, were the nursery quarters, cheerfully furnished in chintz and pale blue. Here were relics of the Princess's one-time nursery : the fruitwood table, an old rocking-horse that had long since lost its tail, and a glass-fronted cabinet containing the glass and china miniatures she had collected in childhood.

The influence of Prince Philip, then a serving naval officer, lay in the pictures, particularly one depicting minesweepers active in moonlight, with seamen of the different periods responding to the beat of Drake's drum.

Ruling firmly over this particular domain was Miss Helen Lightbody from Edinburgh, who had nursed the Duke and Duchess of Gloucester's two sons; assisting her was Miss Mabel Anderson from Perthshire, then still in her twenties. After inserting an advertisement in the 'Situations Wanted' columns of a nurses' magazine, to her astonishment she had been invited for an interview at Buckingham Palace with Princess Elizabeth herself. There she has remained to this day, the adored nanny of the royal offspring: first Prince Charles, then Princess Anne and Prince Andrew and now Prince Edward.

Both Princess Elizabeth and Prince Philip were determined that, during his infancy at least, Charles should be spared the glare of the public spotlight. To most people the experience of growing up is severe enough, but to have one's *gaucheries* flaunted in public would be an impossible strain. Thus it was in saccharine prose that the nation learnt that the Prince surveyed his world from the inordinately long perambulator that had been his mother's; that he referred to his great-grandmother Queen Mary as 'Gan-Gan'; and that he developed a childish obsession for collecting give-away toys from packets of cornflakes.

In those early years the daily routine for Charles was one of rest and play. He was still too young to realize the significance of what had happened when, on a grey and misty day, life unexpectedly changed for him: in the early hours of 6 February 1952 his grandfather King George VI died peacefully in his sleep. At that moment his mother succeeded to the throne as Queen Elizabeth II; he himself, then three years and three months old, at once became the heir apparent. From that moment onwards, until he in turn acquired the crown, he would officially be known as His Royal Highness Prince Charles Philip Arthur George, Duke of Cornwall, Duke of Rothesay, Earl of Carrick, Lord of the Isles and Baron of Renfrew, Prince and Great Steward of Scotland. Not for several more years would the Queen make him Prince of Wales – a title that would automatically admit him as a Knight Companion of the Most Noble Order of the Garter, and Earl of Chester.

When the Queen and the Duke of Edinburgh installed themselves in Buckingham Palace, they occupied apartments on the first and second storeys and arranged a nursery on the floor above. Some notion of Prince Charles's character was beginning to pierce through the childish façade. To a certain extent it was eloquent, too, in his favourite toys: the array of teddy bears and other woolly creatures (with one particular bear and a blue elephant occupying the first place in Charles's affections); the pencils, paints and crayons; the picture books and the toy soldiers. In a neighbouring corridor were parked horse-drawn vehicles, but, rather significantly, toy aircraft and motorcars were usually stored out of sight. Far more popular were two corgis, a hamster named Chi-Chi and a pair of South American love-birds, David and Annie. Even at this tender age Charles was more addicted to animals than to things mechanical. Whenever the technically minded Prince Philip helped his children to assemble model toys, Anne far eclipsed her brother in skill. As Miss Anderson has since expressed, Prince Charles was 'all fingers and thumbs'. Sisterly prowess was again more conspicuous when they were out riding the ponies at Windsor and Balmoral. Since then Charles has been infected by his father's passion for polo, but there is a distinct difference in the way each treats his horses: Charles is said to be decidedly more considerate towards his mounts.

This thoughtfulness towards both people and animals is genuine and innate and has persisted as a pronounced streak in his temperament since childhood. In those sheltered years, his dominant characteristic – according to those who are competent to judge – could be described as 'sweet-natured'. Yet from the occasional photographs that were published in the press, the public were inclined to derive a false impression, assuming that he was a trifle dull. In fact it was an acute serious-mindedness combined with excessive shyness and restraint that led many people to misconstrue the situation. Even today the Prince is reflective and not a little withdrawn, but the rich vein of humour that runs through his character was no less marked in infancy, within the privacy of the domestic environment.

Coupled with his solemn features was the habit of looking with an unflinching gaze, a habit he has never forsaken and one that many today find somewhat disconcerting. His early introspection was accentuated all the more by the pronounced extrovert nature of Princess Anne. When they were driven in public, it was the sister who exuberantly gave the confident wave of the hand. Charles, seeming to shrink into his seat, appeared daunted by the crowd. (How different it was when, years later, they visited Washington. Princess Anne, then nineteen, gave the impression of being harassed and petulant – perhaps with good cause under the irritation of callow American behaviour and questioning – but the resilience under strain that one identifies with royalty was missing: unfortunately she was criticized as 'snobbish, pouting, spoiled, bored, sullen and disdainful'. Charles, in contrast, endeared himself to the Americans [and to the Canadians earlier]. To the delight of many people, he had shed his self-consciousness. An Associated Press report, received by some 1,400 United States newspapers, claimed: 'The

Prince comes out a winner. The Press and apparently the public deemed him charming, sexy and adroit.')

But Charles would tread a difficult path, and one that was frequently painful, before that self-confidence was able to break out, as it were, from its chrysalis of bashfulness. Meanwhile he tended to be a docile boy. Not that he lacked, now and again, fits of temper of the type peculiar to King George VI. But these outbursts were mercurial and brief and were invariably followed by a generous apology. It was, perhaps, the little incidents that pinpointed the Prince's traits: for instance whereas Princess Anne would deliberately stroll past the bear-skinned Palace guards just for the sheer mischievous joy of seeing them present arms, Charles would discreetly admire them from a distance.

His childhood docility was, however, enlivened by the occasional prank. There was, for instance, the incident when he slipped a piece of ice down the collar of a Palace footman. Such occurrences were never overlooked: for every peccadillo the Prince was summarily disciplined, even though some of the Queen's subjects wrote insisting that the heir apparent should be spared corporal punishment. He was not pampered either. Both nannies were staunch advocates of the old-fashioned virtues of discipline, plain cooking and fresh air. A hair mattress was deemed suitable for a monarch in the making, and an electric blanket was taboo; so too was a hot-water bottle, except in times of illness.

In any event Prince Charles is not averse to a little spartanism, relishing, for example, the more rugged aspects of rural life. That is why Balmoral, set amid the fierce grandeur of the Scottish Highlands, has always been his cherished home. Roaming the windy, heather-clad hills, playing ping-pong with the servants in the Silver Pantry, or 'helping' Mr Ronald Aubrey, the chef, to cook, still linger in Charles's mind as the idyllic moments of a blissful childhood.

But in the royal family itself there was the nagging unease that, when eventually he was fully exposed to the cold light of publicity, the heir to the throne might find it unbearably overwhelming. As his governess, the Queen had engaged Miss Catherine Peebles – known as 'Mispy' (Miss P) to the royal children. Born in Glasgow, she completed what has been nicknamed the nursery's 'Scottish Mafia'. It had long been a Palace custom to invite other children to share lessons with the royal pupils. But for Charles the tradition was broken: it was starkly obvious that he would benefit more from being taught alone; progress would be impeded if Charles remained one of a group.

In a frank assessment of her royal charge, Miss Peebles wrote : 'He liked being amused, rather than amusing himself ... He was very responsive to kindness, but if you shouted at him he would draw back into his shell and for a time you would be able to do nothing with him.' This implied that the future of one so hypersensitive would be thorny, if not impossible. And more so in a disruptive, revolutionary age when no established institution evades criticism and when the decline of Britain's influence in the world has stripped the monarchy of its old imperial aura.

All this inevitably imposed an inescapable onus on the heir apparent, to whom, most probably, in days to come many would turn for the lead for which an earlier generation looked in vain to his great-uncle, Edward VIII.

In a world of violent change, revolutionary elements are trying to corrode the pillars of the Establishment and unyielding antagonisms also attempt to undermine the monarchy itself. Hitherto, it was not the institution of monarchy that was the butt of criticism but the propensities and human foibles of the sovereign. Today the situation has been reversed. No one is more sensitively aware than the royal family that the monarchy – as an institution – is now under closer scrutiny than at any time this century. It is its character rather than the titular head that sometimes arouses criticism. This is not hard to understand. Unfairly and inaccurately, cynics present the monarch as a hangover from medievalism, lingering on tenaciously in the twentieth century. The Queen, however, as an individual, personifies and possesses attributes that even her arch-critics cannot justifiably abuse. Moreover to imagine that the Queen is an inarticulate cipher is quite nonsensical : each of the five prime ministers with whom she has so far dealt has at times been made conscious of her personal views and the vigour with which she pursues them. Furthermore, she can derive quiet confidence from the knowledge that she alone can arouse more adulation from the masses – both in Britain and abroad – than all the members of her 'faithful Commons' mustered together.

It is, however, by the way the people know her – and not by the degree of her influence with ministers in the privacy of Buckingham Palace – that they can judge her personality. In an age where vulgarity and low standards tend to be deified, it requires strong qualities of character to uphold old-fashioned traditions that mirror the true facets of civilized human behaviour. Both the Queen and Prince Philip have ratified these by their example.

The problem was to try to guarantee that Prince Charles could do the same. The Queen can never allow herself to forget that one day her son will take her place on the throne and must be equal to the demands in what may be unstable decades to come. Did he have the capacity, the essential dedication and that necessary quality – humility? All this was to be put to the test. Grooming him for his arduous role was about to begin. It would expose him to the most liberal education – sometimes at mental suffering to himself – of any heir apparent in British history.

Long before the time was due, the Queen gave much thought to the education of her eldest son. It was clear that some annealing of Prince Charles's character, to toughen and mould it to the needs of modern kingship, was imperative. The problem was what pattern it should take. In the past royal princes had been entrusted to the dubious care of private tutors, followed by a stint in one of the armed services. As will be explained later, there was much that spoke against this practice; but the system's inherent weakness was its isolation from society – scarcely the ideal training for the present-day world.

By the 1950s the Queen and Prince Philip had reached a decision. Which parent's ideas prevailed, or whether the agreement was mutual, one cannot say. However one suspects – in view of the course that Charles's education eventually took – that the influences and pressures came from Prince Philip. While many fathers like their sons to be virtually a reflection of themselves, the Queen had to think in broader terms. Above all, what were the makings of a future sovereign as well as head of the Commonwealth?

In any event long-standing tradition was cast aside and a revolutionary plan of liberal education – to send Prince Charles to public schools – was embarked upon. One snag was the excessive preoccupation of the media with royal activities. Briefly, how could a young, sensitive boy participate in normal school life if he was constantly pestered by photographers and reporters? Consequently, on 11 April 1955 Commander (now Sir) Richard Colville, the Queen's Press Secretary, wrote to the Newspaper Press Association seeking the collaboration of its members, the national newspapers.

'I am commanded by the Queen [he explained] to say that Her Majesty and the Duke of Edinburgh have decided that their son has reached the stage when he should take part in more grown-up educational pursuits with other children. In consequence, a certain amount of the Duke of Cornwall's instruction will take place outside his home; for example, he will visit museums and other places of interest. The Queen trusts, therefore, that His Royal Highness will be able to enjoy this in the same way as other children without the embarrassment of constant publicity. In this respect Her Majesty feels that it is equally important that those in charge of, or sharing in, the instructions should be spared undue publicity, which can so seriously interrupt their normal lives.

'I would be grateful if you will communicate the above to your members and seek their cooperation in this matter, informing them at the same time that they are at liberty to publish this letter if they so wish.'

The deplorable outcome was that, deprived of facts, newspapermen resorted to their imaginations. No denials or contradictory statements were issued from Buckingham Palace, as this would have contravened a royal custom. But the royal parents were not deflected from their plan. Indeed the lamentable inadequacies of some royal tutors and the calamitous effect on their charges were ample justification for a break with tradition.

Although the Queen herself had escaped tutorial tyranny, she was aware of the unhappiness it had engendered among some of her ancestors. This was bluntly confirmed by Sir Harold Nicolson, the official biographer of King George v, when eventually it was announced that Prince Charles was to be a boarder at a public school. Lecturing in London, he asserted that Edward VII had been educated 'in a most foolish way'; George v had been trained 'in a most ridiculous way'; and that Edward VIII and the Queen's father, George VI, had scarcely been 'educated at all, and I cannot think what their teachers were up to'. His blueprint for the rearing of a modern heir apparent was to 'send him to private school, public school and Oxford'. There is a parallel between Prince Charles and his great-great-grandfather Edward VII in that each had a queen regnant as mother, and a father who meticulously tried, in his own specific way, to be the template in shaping his son's personality. In each instance the results might have been catastrophic. Despite good intentions, the iron rule of Baron Stockmar, who was acclaimed by Queen Victoria and the Prince Consort as the moulder of royal perfection, merely tormented the future Edward VII for years. It is doubtful whether any other British schoolboy laboured so long daily or was stripped of so much leisure. With royal fanaticism, Victoria wanted her son to resemble in every conceivable way the husband she idolized.

Between them the Prince Consort and Stockmar strove to evolve the ideal constitutional monarch and philosopher-king. To the misery of the boy-prince, any childish foible was interpreted as a serious flaw that might threaten his future kingship. When, as a form of defence, Prince Albert Edward brought into play his natural charm, this was instantly frowned upon by the Prince Consort as a quality dangerous in a sovereign. Even the Prince's short stature could not be overlooked and he was duly criticized. Stockmar, whom W. E. Gladstone described as a mischievous old prig, pompously declared : 'A man's education begins the first day of his life.'

Teutonic to the core, humourless, with a wholly abnormal sense of duty – and in temperament quite different from his son – the Prince Consort, concentrating almost solely on books and ignoring the value of experience gained from life, was scarcely a suitable person to prepare his son for the throne. Never, perhaps, in the history of British heirs apparent was there so much instruction for the future.

The astute Lord Melbourne, recognizing the lurking dangers that might arise from an excess of philosophizing, tactfully warned the Queen, 'hoping she would be successful in training and instructing the young Prince of Wales and make him understand his real position and duties and to enable him to withstand the temptations and seduction with which he will find himself beset when he approaches the age of twenty-one'. He further warned that education might 'be able to do much, but it does not do so much as is expected from it. It may mould and direct character, but it rarely alters it.' The Queen foolishly ignored his words.

The education that was prepared so punctiliously for the Prince was abortive for two reasons : not only was it harsh but it debarred any consideration of his character. The Prince's ability to absorb facts or ideas from books was limited, yet all concerned seem to have been unwilling to admit it, starving him of his natural flair to mix with ease, a quality that years later endeared him to the people and endowed him with rare skills in international diplomacy.

In fairness to Victoria and her consort, certain genuine fears did influence the manner in which they educated their eldest son. They feared the spectre of the voluptuous Prince Regent, later the profligate King George IV, an anxiety that strengthened their resolve to instil a sense of duty at an early age. Europe, too, was ravaged by revolution, and the voice of republicanism was growing more strident in Britain. Therefore to Victoria and Albert any aspect of the Prince's character that they assumed to be unpleasant was bound to spell the doom of monarchy.

One would have thought that Prince Albert Edward, having suffered the strain of acute loneliness and segregation in childhood, would have ensured that his own sons, Eddie and George, should be educated with other boys. Their main tutor, the Reverend J. N. Dalton, actually advised this, wishing to take the boys away from the influence of the household's overbearingly social environment thanks to their hedonistic father. Both Prince Albert Edward and Princess Alexandra agreed; strangely, so too did Queen Victoria, although she had 'a great fear of young and carefully brought up Boys mixing with older Boys and indeed with any Boys in general for the mischief done by bad boys and the things they may hear and learn from them cannot be over-rated'. There was also the matter of snobbery, for the Princes' companions would be restricted to the sons of aristocrats. But what she found most repellent of all was that schools, or so she claimed, undermined a boy's affection for his home and shattered his love for his parents and sisters. As a compromise she approved of the Princes' attending Wellington College, simply because the 'infallible' Prince Consort had admired that school. They were not, however, to be allowed to live in; instead they were to reside with their tutor elsewhere.

But the young Princes continued to be confined within the severe limitations of their royal environment, a cramped exclusive world that had a bad effect on them in a scholastic sense. Other than that Prince Albert Edward made certain that his own offspring enjoyed a carefree childhood. One cannot fathom, therefore, why his favourite son, who became the benevolent King George v, should have repeated to some extent the folly of Victoria and the Prince Consort in the education of his own sons. At one point education at a public school was actually considered for Prince Edward – the future Edward viii – but the idea was rejected. Heed was paid to the socialist Keir Hardie who, at the Prince's birth, had predicted that he would 'be surrounded by sycophants and flatterers by the score'. There was certainly some truth in this, but the view that one so young should be safeguarded from the wrong type of boys was quite ridiculous by today's standards. A more tangible reason for not sending him to a public school was that headmasters shrank from accepting responsibility for so important a pupil.

The Reverend H. P. Hansell was therefore chosen for both Edward and his brother Albert, until, like their father before them, they joined the Royal Navy. Mr Hansell emphasized that the absence of both a school atmosphere and the association of boys of a similar age would have a detrimental effect on the sensitive Princes. But again advice went unheeded. Consequently neither was steeled for the traumatic plunge into the hurly-burly of cadet life. Moreover their high social status, rather than inviting respect, inspired taunts and ridicule. Years later Prince Edward, then the Duke of Windsor, gave a glimpse of life in the royal schoolroom. From it one can readily assess how ill trained the Princes were to cope with the pitfalls in a naval community or society generally.

'Constriction [he wrote] was the order of our schoolroom costume. We had a buttoned-up childhood, in every sense of the word. Starched Eton collars invariably encircled our necks and, when old and frayed, cut into our skin like saws. The idea of a boy in short sleeves and an open-necked collar was unthinkable. If, for some special exertion, we were permitted to roll up our sleeves, we must still never loosen our collars and take our coats off. Even with shorts we wore long stockings, right up to our thighs, with never a thought of anything so indelicate as bare knees – except in a kilt.

'In one of my albums I have a photograph of my brother Bertie and me, in a group of a football team of Norfolk village boys. All of us are wearing knickerbockers with long thick stockings – hardly a suitable costume in which to play this strenuous game with freedom.'

It has been claimed that the later clash of temperament between King George V and Prince Edward originated in these childhood experiences. Perhaps it was a factor that encouraged him, as Edward VIII, to lay aside the crown and his kingly destiny, creating an upheaval that might have toppled the throne. Many also believe that the agonizing stammer that tortured Prince Albert, the future George VI, throughout his life worsened under the influence of childhood studies. Doubtless those who planned the education of both Princes entertained the kindliest of intentions, but the pattern was grossly wrong.

The Queen and Prince Philip had resolved that Prince Charles should escape that fate. Already they had assessed the merits and demerits of expert opinion, together with the unsolicited views of left-wing intellectuals who knew best how to educate other people's sons. Since he had been born in an age of social revolution, they argued, it was imperative – if only to follow true democratic principles – that Prince Charles should be admitted to a state school to acquire knowledge of the working classes. The future King Charles III would thus get an insight into the homogeneous world of his future subjects.

While it would be ridiculous to imply that all state schools are 'blackboard jungles', even so the many reports of indiscipline, violence and illiteracy, as well as innumeracy, truancy and the difficulty of conveying ideas to mixed-ability groups that embrace both the clever and the sub-normal hardly assure the right environment for a boy to whom it had so far been necessary to give individual attention. Fervid socialists may find excuses for flaws in the state educational system – or even deny that they exist – but, whatever they contend (irrespective of the relative merits of state education as opposed to the system in the public schools), state education would have been ill suited for a boy of Prince Charles's upbringing and temperament.

While it is essential in modern kingship for a sovereign to be able to communicate with ordinary men, it does not follow that he has to conduct himself like them. Most rational people would neither expect it nor want it. The fact is that a monarch-to-be must receive the training that will shape him into a self-contained being, capable of dealing on equal terms with all classes of men – for instance, heads of state and ambassadors, ministers and commissars, and the hierarchy of trade unions and the Churches, as well as prominent figures in other spheres. It would be unrealistic and unreasonable to do otherwise. To argue that the heir apparent should receive state education like ordinary citizens shrugs off the fact that Prince Charles is no ordinary person and never can be, due to accident of birth.

Events and his mode of living – which differed so vastly from that of other children – must have made this apparent to him since the moment he could comprehend. Notable, for instance, was the day when he observed the ritual of the crowning of his mother in Westminster Abbey. As one writer has explained, Queen Victoria 'was not told about her royal future, but was allowed to discover it for herself from her lessons in history'. Quite sensibly, the process has been reversed in the case of Prince Charles. From infancy the task of kingship that will one day confront him has been gradually but subtly implanted in his mind. In young manhood, on being asked during a radio interview when he first realized as a small boy that he was heir to the throne and 'not just an ordinary chap', he replied: 'I think it's something that dawns on you with the most ghastly inexorable sense. I didn't suddenly wake up in my pram one day and say "Yippee I ..." but I think it just dawns on you slowly that people are interested in one ... and slowly you get the idea that you have a certain duty and responsibility, and I think it is better that way rather than suddenly telling you "You must do this" and "You must do that" because of who you are. I think it is one of those things you grow up in.'

The first major turning-point in Prince Charles's life occurred one afternoon in the late autumn of 1956 when, during tea with the Queen at Buckingham Palace, Colonel Henry Townend, the founder and headmaster of a school at Hill House in Hans Place, Knightsbridge, was asked if he would accept the Prince as one of his pupils. Like others in an earlier reign, Colonel Townend had reservations: there was the unexpected strain of protecting Charles's physical well-being and fear that his presence at Hill House might attract undue press activity, thus seriously affecting the studies of other pupils. But in the end he agreed to the Queen's request.

Secluded from the nearby Knightsbridge traffic, Hans Place, which derives its name from the eminent physician Sir Hans Sloane, is an oval plot of turf bordered by iron railings. Round it rise houses, most of which have been converted into flats, although a sprinkling of private dwellings remain, among them Hill House. Colonel Townend, then forty-seven, an Oxford Blue for Association football, former president of the University Athletic Club, the winner of a gold medal for skiing in Switzerland, and an ex-England athlete, had begun his school four years earlier, basing it on the Swiss system; in short, the curriculum was planned specifically to keep young boys interested and occupied at all times. From the outset, emphasis was placed on punctuality and the need to keep physically fit. Hence the basement's soundproof room – called by pupils 'the padded cell' – with wire over the windows, where the boys could climb ropes, play vigorously with balls and create pandemonium without causing annoyance to anyone.

Boys were admitted between the ages of five and ten and, without question, were the sons of the well-to-do: such people as lawyers and doctors, Army and Navy officers, members of Parliament and diplomats; indeed the latter comprised about one third of the scholars, who came from Europe and further afield. As king (and to some extent as the heir apparent), Charles would be called upon to deal with foreign dignitaries. Hill House afforded him his first opportunity to accustom himself to people from other lands.

The Prince's forthcoming entry to Hill House having leaked to the press, the Queen, trying to protect her exceptionally shy son from the impact of publicity, delayed his arrival at Hill House during the Michaelmas term until 7 November 1956. Charles at that time was not officially enrolled, and attended only in the afternoons to participate in games and acquire some idea of communal activities. It was not until 28 January 1957, at the age of eight, that he started full-time attendance, appearing on the school register as pupil no. 102.

When the facts became known, the cynics criticized the Queen and Prince Philip for not sending the Prince to the nearest state primary school. But apart from the controversial merits of a private school, as that first morning at Hill House made manifestly clear, it would have been virtually impossible in a state school to have guaranteed him an undisturbed environment in which to function. On that January day, every effort had been made for him to arrive inconspicuously at Knightsbridge at twenty-eight minutes past nine – two minutes before the school bell rang. Even so, the cameramen were waiting, instantly recognizing the velvet-collared overcoat with which people were now familiar. To the international press and radio stations Charles's first day at school was a world event, but as photographers were forbidden to photograph aspects of the Prince's school life, the clamour very quickly ceased. The Townends made certain of that, taking it in turn each morning to await the Prince's arrival, not as a formality but as a precaution against the media's encroachment.

Prince Charles was now thrust into a new world (perhaps with traumatic effect) quite different from that of the Palace schoolroom. Hitherto he had lived in a sheltered and restricted backwater, remote from the everyday things that are commonplace to ordinary folk. He had never ridden in a bus, or been inside a shop, or even dealt with money; indeed the significance and value of the coins on which his mother's head appeared had yet to be taught to him. But unlike the princes who became Edward VIII and George VI, he found his companions tolerant, readily admitting the royal newcomer into their circle.

Extremely helpful in this transition was Mrs Townend, a state-registered nurse and one-time theatre sister, at Guy's Hospital, London, to Sir John Weir, who had been in attendance when Prince Charles was born. She taught the Prince elementary anatomy, first aid and general knowledge.

Colonel Townend, who was addressed at all times as 'Sir', taught Latin (a new subject for Charles), French and geography, and also instructed the boys in Association football, although generally academic subjects had preference in the curriculum over sport. All the male members of the teaching staff – known as 'tutors' – wore white shirts, blazers and flannel trousers; the female tutors taught the younger pupils. Each tutor had charge of about nine boys, thus ensuring more intensive instruction for each pupil. Slovenliness, in either appearance or deportment, was never tolerated. Self-discipline and the ability to accept responsibility were carefully nurtured, helping Charles to try to counter his shyness. Swimming was taught at Chelsea Baths (although Charles's father had already given him lessons in the Palace pool) and, marching two abreast, the boys would cross nearby King's Road, proceeding to the grounds of the Duke of York's Headquarters, the Chelsea military depot, for soccer. Passers-by never knew that the heir apparent was among them. That was what the Queen and Prince Philip had always intended. In school the Prince received no privileges and, as was the practice at Buckingham Palace – even among the staff – he was called Charles by his school-fellows and Prince Charles by his tutors. When the Queen and Prince Philip attended sports day they too insisted on being treated like ordinary parents, without formality.

After the serenity of the Palace schoolroom Prince Charles had been bewildered on his initiation to Hill House, but his first school report reflected progress and ran: 'Lent 1957, Upper VI. *Reading* – Very good indeed. Good expression. *Writing* – Good. Firm, clear, well formed. *Arithmetic* – Below form average. Careful but slow – not very keen. *Scripture* – Shows keen interest. *Geography* – Good. *History* – Loves this subject. *French* – Shows promise. *Latin* – Made a fair start. *Art* – Good, and simply loves drawing and painting. *Singing* – A sweet voice, especially in lower register. *Football* – Enjoying the game. *Gymnastics* – Good.'

Today it can be seen that this first report crystallized the Prince's enthusiasms in later life. In young manhood he is an avid reader when he can find the time; in fact, Lord Butler, Master of Trinity College, Cambridge, has disclosed that Prince Charles 'has a tremendous affinity for books'. Moreover, he still retains his profound interest in the Scriptures and, like the Queen, believes fervently in the Christian faith. Once he confided to a friend that, but for the fact that he was destined to become the secular head of the Anglican Church, he would like to identify himself with a religion that combined the Christian moral code with Buddhism's respect for nature. (On this point one wonders what compromise he could reach between his love of game shooting and Buddhist principles.) His zeal for music has not waned. Having sung Bach's Mass in B minor in a large choir, he said with enthusiasm that the experience was incomparable : 'I do not know whether it is the volume of the voices, or the sense of participation – you are not just listening, you are helping to make the sound – but it is really very exciting. Yet it is something you can enjoy only if you keep at it. You cannot just turn up and say : "I like singing in choirs. Can I sing in yours tonight, please?" '

That first school report had signified Prince Charles's penchant for history and art. His keenness for both – but particularly history – has never diminished. Today he can say :

'I have always been interested in history, even when I was quite small. I do not know whether it is me, or being born into what I was, but I feel history. It fascinates me. I am a romantic at heart, really. At Gordonstoun I was very keen on it, and when the time came for me to go to Cambridge, and choose my subjects, I thought: now here is a chance I will never have again – to do some *pre*-history, get to know about the earlier societies, and the most primitive kinds of men. When you meet as many people as I do, from different countries, different colours, different stages of social development, with different drives, you become curious about what makes men tick, and what makes different men tick differently. You wonder about the fundamental tension in a man, in mankind, between body and soul. I got on to this at Gordonstoun and I grabbed the chance to follow it up a bit at Cambridge.'

Art was the Prince's favourite subject at Hill House, where drawing was greatly encouraged. Perhaps more than anything else, it helped him to make the great adjustment and attune himself to the communal life of a school, for drawing and painting had been a popular pastime in the Palace nursery. On his first day at Hill House he had painted his impression of the royal yacht *Britannia* at Tower Bridge. As in the case of the Duke of Edinburgh, in adult life painting is not only a recreation but an intensive study. His current penchant is for watercolours, which he finds 'very difficult but most rewarding'.

During his second term – as in the first – the Prince suffered a further bout of tonsillitis. On this occasion the affected organs were removed at Buckingham Palace and, responding to the Prince's request, the surgeon preserved them in spirit for display to visitors to the nursery. After a convalescence lasting three weeks, Prince Charles returned to his light oak, steel-framed desk at Hill House. Drawing and painting continued to be his foremost talent and arithmetic his scholastic nightmare. That Charles did not grapple very skilfully with the complexities of the science of numbers did not worry the Queen unduly. In her own childhood the subject had been a schoolroom incubus. But mathematics would never be a facet of kingship and the Queen was more concerned that the heir apparent should be adept when dealing with all manner of men.

When August came Prince Charles had discarded his Hill House uniform of cinnamon-coloured sweater, shorts, blazer and cap. For the royal pupil, the school in Hans Place had fulfilled its function: to rid the Prince of at least some of his shyness and smooth the way for the second stage of his education. In the autumn Prince Charles would set off for another school, this time away from the protective Palace atmosphere for a term at a time. At Hill House he would leave behind a memento of his days there: a little square stool, five inches tall, on which he sat on Friday evenings, taking tea with Mrs Townend until the chauffeur came to drive him to Windsor Castle for the weekend. Today, on an honours board in the school hall, simple words tell how a king in the making donned the Hill House uniform – attending a London day-school as no other future monarch had ever done before.

2 The Years at Cheam

It is an irony that, perhaps of all the people in the land, the Head of State should find it the most difficult when choosing an educational establishment for the heir apparent. There are the normal factors to bear in mind : the pupil's temperament and his ability to dovetail into the activities of a specific school; the type of curriculum and whether it and the teaching staff can develop the right qualities needed for kingship. Last but by no means least, there are the impassioned outbursts that – depending on the nature of her decision – the Queen would have to contend with.

On and off, there had already been controversial tussles over the Prince's future for some time; the topic had aroused far deeper feelings than in more immediate reigns. Some people wished, without further ado, to pluck Prince Charles from his rarefied height and deposit him in what was to them a more realistic world among the less privileged. This was the age of the common man, they ranted, and the more vociferous members of the more liberal circles in society bluntly made certain that the Queen and Prince Philip were conscious of it.

Such a person was the second Lord Altrincham, whose egalitarianism caused him to discard his title and be known simply as Mr John Grigg. Although an old Etonian himself – achieving in his day the coveted rank of Captain of the Oppidans – he vehemently criticized the value of being taught in a public school. Others clearly echoed his views. His lordship, who edited a small circulation political monthly, *National and English Review*, triggered off the sharpest altercation because his writings centred on the monarchy. There should be no question, he wrote : Prince Charles should be sent to a state primary school.

The royal family had felt the cool breeze of social change wafting through the Palace windows. They knew that the need for change was timely, but to what extent? After receiving lessons at Buckingham Palace from private tutors, Edward VIII and George VI had been trained as naval cadets at Osborne and Dartmouth. Neither had experienced life at a normal school, and nor, for that matter, had the Queen herself. She, too, had been educated behind what has been aptly described as 'the traditional royal stockade of governesses and special teachers brought in from outside'. Foremost among these had been Mr (later Sir) C. H. K. Marten, a future Provost of Eton, who, defending what struck many people as the harsh system of casting a boy into a public school from sheltered home life, stressed that the system had grown humane by introducing the preparatory school.

Harsh or humane, this would be the fate of Prince Charles, but again the question arose: which school? To reach her decision the Queen made ostensibly casual visits to certain schools, quietly assessing the suitability of each. All the while the Queen's movements came under the keen scrutiny of the press, who made their own predictions. Schoolmasters were also invited to Her Majesty's informal luncheon parties at Buckingham Palace.

But in the end it was an old boy of Cheam School who influenced the Queen's mind: Charles, it was decided, should become a pupil at his father's one-time prep school. The diehards, accustomed to a prince following the traditional routine, viewed the choice with distaste and gloom.

In retrospect, it seems quite obvious that Prince Philip prepared the blueprint of his son's schooling; indeed in due course the heir apparent would be boarded at two establishments that the Duke himself had attended: Cheam and Gordonstoun. Commenting recently on that educational programme, Prince Charles emphasizes that he was never coerced into slavishly emulating his father: 'His [Prince Philip's] attitude was very simple: he told me what were the pros and cons of all the possibilities and attractions and told me what he thought best because I had come to see how wise he was. By the time I had to be educated, I had perfect confidence in my father's judgement. When children are young, of course you have to decide for them. How can they decide for themselves?'

Cheam School, standing in sixty-five acres of grounds on the Berkshire border, had long been connected with the Mountbatten family, to which the Duke of Edinburgh belongs. The association originated in 1914, when Prince Louis of Battenberg, the Duke's grandfather, was then First Sea Lord. Two midshipmen had favourably surprised him by their aplomb. Learning that they were ex-pupils of Cheam, he promptly decided that the male members of his family should enrol there from now on.

The school has deep roots, stretching back to the reign of Charles I, for its old boys were matriculating at Oxford and Cambridge even during the Civil War. In 1665, when Charles II was on the throne, the Rev George Aldritch, who maintained a little school in London for the sons of aristocrats, fled from the Great Plague and with his noble scholars sought sanctuary in the Surrey market-town of Cheam. There, in the High Street, they shared a house called White-hall with a local school. Cheam School's reputation grew and the names of aristocratic sons were registered immediately after they had been christened; by 1719 it occupied new premises in Cheam, among elm trees and thirteen acres of land. In 1934, to escape from a new railway station and encroaching urbanization, Cheam School moved yet again, this time to Headley on the Berkshire Downs, though it still retained the name of Cheam.

Like many ancient establishments, Cheam has had a somewhat chequered career. The register contained the names of fifteen scholars when, in 1752, William Gilpin bought the school. With his arrival came reform.

To the eighteenth-century mind it was thought to be essential to beat learning into boys. Gilpin, however, was loath to flog, deciding instead on a fitting punishment for a specific offence. Fines or detention in varying degrees, and physical exercise, formed the basis of his code. Only in extreme cases was the birch inflicted – and then rarely. Gilpin, who may have been the model for Smollett's school-master in *Peregrine Pickle*, was otherwise known as 'Dr Syntax'.

In 1855 Cheam was reorganized by a headmaster named Tabor, who was apparently highly sensitive to rank. A peer was addressed as 'my darling child', the son of a peer was referred to as 'my dear boy' and a commoner was called 'my child'. It would be fascinating to know how he would have addressed Prince Charles.

Cheam claims to be England's oldest preparatory school, so not unexpectedly some distinguished names are written in its register. That of Thomas Pepys, cousin of Samuel, the famous diarist, is there. So, too, is that of Lord Randolph Churchill who, according to Sir Winston, his even more illustrious son, was 'most kindly treated and quite content'. One can visualize Lord Randolph, accompanied by the future Lords Donoughmore and Aberdeen, bowling along at

Cheam in a four-in-hand. The school's ex-pupils also include two former viceroys of India, Lord Willingdon and Lord Hardinge of Penshurst, as well as two speakers of the House of Commons : Henry Addington (later Viscount Sidmouth), who by means of the Treaty of Amiens ended the war with France in 1802; and Colonel Clifton-Brown (subsequently Viscount Ruffside). Lord Dunsany, the Irish writer, and Sir Ian Hamilton, military commander-in-chief at the disastrous Gallipoli landing, were also at Cheam. Prince Philip and his cousin, the Marquess of Milford Haven, had been among the last of the scholars before the migration from Surrey.

At the tercentenary celebrations in 1947, not long before his marriage, Prince Philip introduced Princess Elizabeth, as the Queen then was, to a former headmaster, the Rev Harold Taylor, remarking: 'This is my late headmaster, who used to cane me.' Years later, during his Australian tour, Prince Charles would recall a similar painful incident. By chance he met a former schoolfriend, Philip Beck, now a journalist, the son of Mr Peter Beck, who shared the duties of joint headmaster with Mr Mark Wheeler. The royal visitor was then inspecting the operation of a paper-mill in Hobart, Tasmania. 'I remember your father well,' recalled the Prince. 'He caned me once – no – twice.' The canings had been for ragging. Prince Charles also remembered May, Beck's sister, who had been a member of the Prince's class – 'and always got much better marks than the rest of us'.

Other memories are deeply etched on the Prince's mind, not the least being the nervous tension as September approached in 1957 and he was about to depart for Cheam. Miss Mabel Anderson has since revealed that for Prince Charles home life has always had magnetic appeal; that he 'felt family separation very deeply. He dreaded going away to school.'

Centuries ago it was not uncommon for the heir apparent to live apart from his parents, even in childhood, and be the focal point in a court of his own. Now in young manhood Prince Charles will eventually set up his own household and live at Chevening, the picturesque estate bequeathed by the late Lord Stanhope as a home for the Prince of Wales. One wonders if he welcomes this with any great enthusiasm, considering that when in London he is quite content with his three-room suite on the second floor of Buckingham Palace. The sitting-room, overlooking a gravelled forecourt, is of modest dimensions. Here pale blue curtains merge elegantly with the yellow and tan of a sofa and leather armchairs. Shelves of books reflect his enthusiasm for history, archaeology and art. On the coffee-table lie colourfully illustrated volumes on polo and the eighteenth century, but even more arresting is Charles's collection of Eskimo carvings, including a massive musk-ox. Quite commendably, unlike so many of his contemporaries, Prince Charles admits unashamedly: 'I have never wanted not to have a home life – to get away from home. I love my home life. We happen to be a very close-knit family. I am happier at home with the family than anywhere else.'

Drawn intensely to his domestic environment, the young Prince 'shuddered with apprehension' on that September day when he began the journey from Balmoral to Cheam. An earlier prince had remarked likewise: the last heir apparent was tortured by similar fears on contemplating departure from the Palace nursery to Osborne.

'Meanwhile [he wrote in *A Family Album*] I was to face the alarming experience of going to school. The regulations of those Naval colleges at Osborne and Dartmouth were to condemn me, together with some hundreds of fellow cadets, to a stretch of four long years of boyhood in uniform, spent partly in quarters which had once been Queen Victoria's stables. The wardrobe – or "gear" as I soon learnt to call it – with which I must now, at the age of twelve and a half, be equipped ...'

The Queen and Prince Philip travelled with Prince Charles on the overnight train journey, followed by a sixty-mile car drive to Headley. But the parents did not remain long at Cheam: it was the beginning of term, with its customary pandemonium and bustle. With rather startling abruptness the diffident, chubby little newcomer – 'notably in need of a haircut' – realized that he was alone, and miserable. He was the cynosure of scores of young eyes, the butt of curiosity, there to survive or fall in the rough and tumble of a boarding-school.

The other boys had already been warned that, in the new school year, one of their fellows would be the future King of England. During the holidays Mr Beck had written to their parents informing them that it was 'the wish of the Queen and Prince Philip that there shall be no alteration in the way the school is run and that Prince Charles shall be treated the same as other boys ... It will be a great help if you will explain this. The staff will call him and refer to him as Prince Charles, but the boys will call him Charles ... His parents' wishes are that he should be given exactly the same education and upbringing as other boys in the school.' But by any standards a future monarch is no ordinary boy, and the other pupils knew that only too well. Hence the hesitancy to form friendships. But loneliness, according to Lord Louis Mountbatten, Prince Charles's greatuncle, 'is something that royal children have always suffered from and always will: not much you can do about it'. Recalling his own boyhood experiences, he is on record as saying: 'When I was at school I had the title of prince and that was quite enough to put people off. It is always the undesirable types who try to make up to you: the ones you really like tend to steer clear in case they are accused of being snobs.'

Prince Charles was neither flamboyant nor extrovert by temperament (and perhaps a trifle conscious of his aura of rank), and in his earlier years it took him (in the words of Miss Anderson) a long time to realize that some people might be especially nice to him simply because of his status: 'Princess Anne was always a much quicker judge of character that way; she was far more inclined to take people at their face value. I do not think it occurred to him that people could be so unkind as to pretend to like him, when all they were really after was some kind of social advantage.'

In those early weeks at Cheam, Charles managed to hide his inner feelings with a semblance of outward composure. Maybe this was attributable to his royal training. It is said that at his first Sunday morning church parade he was inwardly irked by the sniggers when the vicar offered prayers for the royal family, specifically drawing attention to the Duke of Cornwall. Within weeks, however, he had fitted himself tolerably well into school routine. He now slept in a dormitory with schoolfellows, itself an unusual experience. Save that of the senior boy, all the two-centuries-old beds were springless and, like the carpeted floor, of solid wood. In wintertime, until late afternoon, in this austere little world of bare floor and unresponsive hair mattresses, the windows were kept open despite the chill air. At four o'clock they were closed, and the doors were opened, leaving the warm air to rise from the main boiler-room below.

Each morning at a quarter past seven the school burst into life. First the boys made their beds; then came washing and dressing – grey suits with short trousers – and being inspected for tidiness by the matron before prayers, followed by a formal handshake with one of the headmasters. Breakfast was taken at eight o'clock when, according to the rota, each boy waited at table. An hour was allowed for the meal, then, but for a short break for milk, lessons went on unbroken until lunchtime, at one o'clock. Afternoons were a mixture of games and two more lessons then, under the unflinching gaze of three stags' heads and a fox mask, the pupils ate high tea at six o'clock. For the older pupils there was still an hour's 'prep' before lights were put out soon after eight. No lessons were arranged in the afternoon on Wednesdays and Saturdays and Prince Charles, like the rest of the pupils, welcomed the extra half-hour in bed before church parade on Sundays. Each night he cleaned his own shoes and helped to keep the form-room tidy.

The boys kept their clothes in wicker baskets, which were more commonly known as 'dog baskets'. They were expected to send at least one letter home each week. Stationery and other necessities could be purchased in a little room called 'the bank'; sweets were also stocked here, but there was a maximum of half a pound per boy each week. Pocket money was also restricted. As Duke of Cornwall, Charles was doubtless one of the wealthiest children alive, yet his affluence was never allowed to intrude into the workings of Cheam. Even so, the genuinely kind-hearted Prince liked at times to spend his limited funds on his friends. Somehow this leaked to the press. The result was a false and contemptible story: Prince Charles, it was alleged, was deliberately deprived of cash and had been forced to sell personal possessions to defray the cost of a clandestine party after lights out. The story was patently false, but it sufficed to melt the hearts of delegates to the Retail Candy Stores Institute of America, then in conference in San Francisco. Addressed to H.R.H. Prince Charles at Cheam, there came across the Atlantic riches galore for the boys: tootsie rolls and bubble gum, an eye-boggling assortment of chocolates and lollipops, fruit-flavoured jelly beans and peanut butter in good measure. 'We were told the Prince was short of candy, so our committee unanimously passed a resolution to the effect that we ought to pitch in and help him out of a jam,' ran an accompanying note.

Kind though the gesture had been, the news-agency that had disseminated the falsehood highlighted an unpleasant facet of the press. During the Prince's first term a detective had been installed in a cottage in the school grounds to deal swiftly with intruders. Despite this, stories relating to Prince Charles appeared in the national newspapers on sixty-eight out of a possible eighty-eight days. It seems incredible that the national press – not to mention scurrilous publications abroad – resorted to so much effort and guile to record the normal innocent activities of a plump little schoolboy. At first it was assumed – quite wrongly, as time would prove – that this spate of stories was being extracted from among pupils, parents and teaching staff. Relationships at school were in danger of being fouled by suspicion – a threat that could not be allowed to continue during the Prince's four-year stay.

Accordingly Commander Richard Colville, the Queen's Press Secretary, invited London newspaper editors to Buckingham Palace during the Christmas holidays. There Mr Peter Beck described to them the disruptive influence that the uncontrolled imagination of newsmen and their constant surveillance were having on the school. Bribes had even been offered for reports about the Prince. Commander Colville therefore made it clear to all that unless the persecution ceased, the Queen proposed to end the Prince's stay at Cheam and have him taught privately by tutors. This was imperative not only for her son but also for the other pupils at Cheam.

The irresponsibility of the British press diminished at once, but security could not be lessened: there were still the cranks and the eccentrics to counter, and the curious who gravitated idly to Headley at weekends, hoping to catch a glimpse of the Prince.

One night a detective roused one of the headmasters, warning him that a figure had been seen acting furtively on the school roof. Immediately all the pupils and staff were alerted and the roof was searched, but no one was traced. To make the situation more puzzling, nobody was seen to be absent from the dormitories. Some time elapsed before the mystery was solved: a pupil called Daukes admitted to being the culprit, having reached his dormitory just before the search was made.

Foreign photographers represented the worst of the nuisances, to the extent that security had to be increased. A number even climbed the school walls during darkness to secrete themselves in the woods and undergrowth with long-range cameras until daybreak. Supervision was also intensified by the teaching staff themselves, who had heard movement in the darkness after the daytime guard had gone off duty. Police supervision was therefore at its greatest between dusk and dawn.

In November 1959 a more serious menace arose, making supervision even more imperative. A number of men and women who had quit the Irish Republican Army had banded together to form what was known as the Fianna Uladh or 'Warriors of Ulster'. It seems that the security authorities had been warned of an Irish plan to kidnap Prince Charles as a means of bringing partition to an end. The American newspapers quoted a confidential message that purported to have been sent from Scotland Yard to British newspaper editors. It was rumoured that in the Irish community living in the Kilburn district of London, the police had arrested a one-time Warrior, who, having fled from Belfast, had exposed the plot.

In general, security measures functioned smoothly, without disrupting the life of the school. The worst that befell anyone was the occasional punishment. As well as caning, as in Mr Gilpin's time, there were recognized punishments, varying from a reprimand from one of the headmasters to being deprived of attending the Saturday-night cinema. However, there were also inducements to pupils to apply themselves more industriously and to display enterprise; merit was rewarded with small financial payments credited to a savings account and withdrawn by the successful pupils when they left school.

The primary aim at Cheam was to make certain that the boys attained the necessary proficiency to secure a place at a public school. Instead of the normal house system of independent schools, Cheam is split into four sections christened after Commonwealth countries: Canada, Australia, New Zealand and, during Charles's sojourn there, South Africa. Curiously, forms are numbered in reverse order to those at other schools, so that Prince Charles started in form VII and ended in IB. The pattern of results that gradually emerged was, more or less, a carbon copy of that at Hill House.

To the future King of England the subject of mathematics was still the bogey of the blackboard. Pupil and master, Mr David Muir, tussled heroically with a tangle of figures that brought only sorrow to both. Once more it was clear that history and art were the Prince's forte. History to Charles was not the mouldering bones of past ages, but a vivid kaleidoscope of events affecting the lives of men and reaching by their influence down the centuries. History is vital to Prince Charles because he has long known that he himself is part of the nation's history. As Mr Dermot Morrah wrote: 'Later it came to have another, less comfortable, significance. He began to realise that history, which in the text-books is about his ancestors, will one day be about him. There have been times when he has been oppressed by the thought that some casual action may get confused with national affairs, that when he writes an informal letter to his mother or a friend it may somehow get swept up in the archives and provide raw material for some future historian.'

The drastic transmutation from the warm, domestic scene to community life at Cheam resulted in moments of unhappiness. To some extent such times were assuaged by music. He sang in the choir at school services at Headley Church and began to play the piano. Years later, commenting on his musical endeavours both at Cheam and Gordonstoun, he said :

'When I went to my prep school, I learned the piano. No good. Then I took up the trumpet. I rather enjoyed it, but one of the music teachers, who happened to be German, didn't. She could not stand the noise. I used to play the trumpet in the school orchestra. We made such an awful noise in the back row. I can hear the music teacher now. We would all be playing away and making a hell of a din, and suddenly she couldn't stand it any longer, and she would put down her violin and we would all stop and she would shout – she had a heavy German accent and somehow that made her sound more agonised – "Ach! Zoze trumpetz! Ach! Zoze trumpetz! Stawp zoze trumpetz!" So I gave up my trumpet. Later I began to think about the 'cello. It had such a deep rich sound. One night I was at the Festival Hall and I heard Jacqueline Dupré playing with her husband, Daniel Barenboim. I had never heard sounds like it. I said : "I must try this." So I did. I couldn't keep it up. I remember playing in a performance of Beethoven's Fifth one night. It was a wonderful experience, but I couldn't play concentratedly enough to avoid being confused.'

At Cheam he was still under the spell of drawing and painting, showing his work at the school exhibition, and it was also at Cheam that his latent sense of the theatrical was awakened. He played the Duke of Gloucester (subsequently Richard III) in a school play, *The Last Baron*, when the pupil who was chosen for the part left Cheam unexpectedly. On that school stage Charles was recalling history, depicting one of the Queen's predecessors (in the collateral sense). He was eulogized for his performance. Without any trace of sycophancy, the dramatic critic of the *Cheam School Chronicle* wrote : 'Prince Charles played the traditional Gloucester with competence and depth : he had a good voice and excellent elocution, and very well conveyed the ambition and bitterness of the twisted hunchback.'

At least he had exhibited one skill that surpassed that of his father. By going to Cheam, Charles constantly lived in the shadow of the Duke of Edinburgh. There was always the daunting, mind-nagging truth that his assertive father had achieved distinction in the first eleven in football, rugby and cricket. Charles's achievement in team games was decidedly modest. In cricket, he played regularly in the second team and occasionally in the first, being more accomplished at soccer than rugger and protesting that in the latter 'they always put me in the second row – the worst place in the scrum'. In his final year he captained the first football team and although their failure may not be attributable to his captaincy that ill-fated side lost every match. Maybe Cheam was currently lacking in talent, but in the school magazine someone censured: 'At half, Prince Charles seldom drove himself as hard as his ability and position demanded.'

It is on record that an educationalist summed up Cheam's objective as an attempt to evolve 'a happy boy rather than a brilliant one'. That being so, this illustrious prep school was not wholly successful in the case of Prince Charles. Cheam did not apparently fill the Prince with ecstasy, but then no phase of his school life wholly endeared itself to him. In an assessment of his royal charge, Mr Peter Beck has described him as above average in intelligence but only average in attainment. From this one should not deduce that the Prince was highly intelligent but indolent. Intense conscientiousness (also a trait of the Queen) is the hallmark of whatever he endeavours to achieve. Mr Beck merely meant that the Prince, with an insatiable thirst for facts (a characteristic of the Duke of Edinburgh), possessed a far greater store of general knowledge than most of his contemporaries – an attribute that, as it has been pointed out, is more in keeping with the requirements of the Act of Settlement by which the Prince will one day reign as King Charles III.

That Charles's academic star did not scintillate unduly at Cheam did not cause either the Queen or Prince Philip to suffer paroxysms of hysteria. There was no need to be alarmed. Even a prince could be a slow developer and there was ample evidence to confirm that academic sluggishness did not necessarily herald intellectual incapacity in later life. At Harrow, for example, there had been nothing to presage future Churchillian stature, and if one wanted to look more closely inside the family there was confidence to be drawn from the example of Lord Louis Mountbatten. On his own admission, he 'began life rather unbright. I was a very slow starter indeed – but I consider that starting slowly is a very solid and sound way of getting there in the end: it helps you to develop a very feet-on-the-ground approach to life.'

Unfortunately for the young Prince's ego, the news that emanated from Cheam was misconstrued. Without any basis for their assumptions, some people wrongly imagined that Prince Charles's unspectacular days at preparatory school could mean only one thing: he was slow to comprehend and perhaps even a little backward. Away from school he was sometimes seen in the wake of his talented father, slavishly copying his mannerisms, though rather unconvincingly. Hence the mistaken belief that he lacked individuality.

It was the price he paid for being born into royalty. But the innuendoes bit deeply into his sensitivity and for a long time left their scars. What was interpreted as dullness was, if anything, nothing more than an acute awareness of his status and a consciousness of being under the public gaze; as a result he took both himself and life too seriously. Unable to retaliate or deny, yet knowing that what was said or written was grossly inaccurate, he would sometimes be unable to stem the boyhood tears after reading cruel comments in the press. It seemed that no allowance was to be made for his sheltered upbringing, and whereas the Queen's humblest subject could make mistakes without ridicule or comment, what appeared to be the slightest error on the Prince's part resulted in a spate of worldwide headlines.

For a time the absurd treatment that he received from certain elements of the press evoked his distrust and dislike. Furthermore, it was a long while before it vanished. Now in more mature years he can accept the situation philosophically. He does, however, make a clear distinction between the 'real gentlemen of the press' and those who are not so gentlemanly – 'a considerable number to whom the word is less applicable'. Obviously when he has the choice he prefers to deal with the former. Referring to his boyhood reaction to unfair criticism, he has admitted that he was sometimes roused to anger, adding:

'... then, as I got older, I tried to think it out. I knew I must not go on being cross, or shouting at people – it wasn't becoming in one so young. So I tried to understand the other person's position and put myself in his shoes. Part of that means recognising the demands a newspaper makes on all the people who work in it – even if they own it. Anyway, it is when nobody wants to write about you or take a photograph of you that you ought to worry in my sort of job. Then there would be no great point in being around. And I could not stand being around if there didn't seem to be any point to it.'

3 'There is More in You'

On the evening of 23 January 1962 a simple announcement from Buckingham Palace revealed without any trace of fuss that Prince Charles would take up residence at Gordonstoun when the summer term opened on 1 May. Until then there had been speculation as to the choice of school, interjected with controversial outbreaks over the comparative merits of public schools and the state comprehensive system. At his birth the name of Prince Charles had been entered at Eton College, not because it was Britain's premier independent school but because of precedent: the first member of the royal family to be educated at a boarding-school had been the Duke of Gloucester, who in turn had decided on Eton for his sons, Prince William and Prince Richard. Another Old Etonian was Sir David Bowes-Lyon, brother of the Queen Mother. Other than Gordonstoun, whose most famous old boy was Prince Philip himself, Eton was the royal family's sole link with the public-school system.

But to left-wing and other biased elements Eton was synonymous with privilege, the prerogative of rich men's sons. There could be scant argument against this: the original purpose for which public schools had been founded – to provide education for clever but poor boys – had long since vanished behind the cheque books of the affluent. The inception of Eton itself had been the outcome of Henry VI's altruistic desire to take twenty-five indigent boys, instructing that 'no Eton scholar shall grow long hair, or a beard, or wear peaked shoes'. Schools like Eton, clamoured the critics, created an insurmountable class barrier, whereas the proud boast of the monarchy was that it was classless. That the essence of teaching talent and the superb quality of education could equip the heir apparent far more competently for his future role appeared to be of little consequence. They were also happy to ignore the fact that one reform, a scheme to absorb a percentage of working-class boys into public schools, had been virtually abortive.

When the Queen and Prince Philip, and the Queen Mother, visited Eton in 1960 it was therefore generally assumed that this breeding-ground of so many prime ministers and cabinet ministers would be the next stage of Prince Charles's education. Some people viewed with disquiet the prospect one day of an Old Etonian alliance between crown and cabinet. Lord Altrincham contended that the Prince should put stress on the study of languages, notably Russian and Hindi, failing to appreciate that neither language was taught in the majority of the schools of which he was an ardent devotee.

With justification, advocates of the independent schools put emphasis on discipline, Christian teaching and willingness to accept responsibility – qualities that were imperative in kingship. But they did not necessarily recommend Eton as the wisest choice. Instead the names of Westminster, Winchester (where, someone remarked, Charles might find himself in the same dormitory as half the future socialist cabinet), Milton Abbey, Trinity College in Perthshire and Charterhouse cropped up.

At one point the Prince himself favoured the latter, so that he could renew friendships with boys from Cheam. Eton also had its attractions, partly because friends were there and – an important point for the home-loving Prince – the college was just over the bridge from Windsor Castle and within easy reach of Buckingham Palace.

But that was just the reason why Eton could never be contemplated. After the experience at Cheam, Eton was unquestionably much too vulnerable to the ubiquitous mass media in London; it would have been unreasonable to subject either the Prince or the college authorities to the exasperation of constant intrusion. Doubtless the Duke of Edinburgh again influenced the Queen in her final choice. It is natural that, like many fathers, Prince Philip wished to foster his own inclinations in the Prince of Wales. Maybe he reasoned that the austerities at Gordonstoun might mould his son in the likeness of his ebullient self and cure him of his introspection. But it was a gamble that could have been an insensitive exercise with unfortunate results, for although Prince Charles may be inclined to hero-worship his father, there are considerable differences in their dispositions. It requires little observation to appreciate that Princess Anne is more akin in temperament to Prince Philip, whereas in Prince Charles one notes some of the marked characteristics of George vi, his grandfather. Perhaps that is why the Prince of Wales is the Queen Mother's favourite grandchild; between them there is a great affinity.

At that age the Prince of Wales seemed to lack the resilience to cope with the rigours of Gordonstoun. Dr Kurt Hahn, the founder, had described his school as one where 'the sons of the powerful' could be 'emancipated from the prison of privilege'. But emancipation of that type can be an astringent process to anyone who is ill suited to it by nature. Some boys would have resented it bitterly. Prince Charles had already drawn his own conclusion that Gordonstoun 'sounded pretty gruesome', but, although there is stubbornness in his make-up, he is not of that breed that easily revolts. Today he insists: 'I am not a rebel by temperament. I do not get a kick out of not doing what is expected of me, or of doing what is not expected of me. I do not feel an urge to react against older people. I have been brought up with older people and I have enjoyed it. On the whole in my youth I preferred to be with older people. I have observed my father's wisdom and judgement and appreciate it, and benefited from it.' In that way he escaped many of the imbecilities so often associated with adolescence.

No matter what has been written or said, the fact is that the final decision as to whether he should go to Gordonstoun or to some other school was his. But his reliance on his father's judgement, coupled with an unerring sense of duty, induced him to agree. At the same time, the prospect was one he never cherished. In his young mind there were the stories of the severities of Dr Hahn's establishment, plus the fact that, in his own day, Prince Philip had excelled at Gordonstoun.

'When Philip came to Gordonstoun [wrote Hahn], his most marked trait was his undefeatable spirit. He felt the emotions of both joy and sadness deeply, and the way he looked and the way he moved indicated what he felt. That even applied to the minor disappointments in a schoolboy's life. His laughter was heard everywhere. He had inherited from his Danish family the capacity to derive great fun from small incidents. In his school work he showed a lively intelligence. In community life, once he made a task his own, he showed meticulous attention to detail and pride of workmanship which was never content with mediocre results.'

But that related to Prince Philip. Would the same tenacity be exhibited by his son?

Lord Louis Mountbatten has confirmed that the Prince of Wales positively disliked Gordonstoun at first: 'It is a tough school and he doesn't like tough things when he first embarks on them. He is not the type to rush into something with an easy, short-lived enthusiasm: instead, he lives with it, comes to grips with it, and ends up doing very well at it.'

Eton, in the views of critics, had been unsuitable because it mirrored the Establishment. Now the 'Gordonstoun system' was condemned because, it was argued, its credo was to foster a class that was essentially élitist. Gordonstoun was based on a school that was brought into being in 1920 by Prince Max von Baden in his castle-monastery at Salem on Lake Constance, in southern Germany. The last chancellor of the Hohenzollern empire, he had striven to raise his country from the debris of the First World War by trying to create a new form of leadership – briefing his staff to build 'up the imagination of the boy of decision and the will-power of the dreamer so that in future wise men will have the nerve to lead the way they have shown, and men of action will have the vision to imagine the consequences of their decisions'.

Briefly, the object was to replace the loathsome Prussian *Junker* with 'soldiers who, at the same time, are lovers of peace'. Prince Max appointed Dr Hahn, his former private secretary, to supervise this unique venture. Although the Hahn system was born in Bavaria, it was partly inspired by the stamina bred in British public schools. Years earlier it had been claimed that Waterloo had been won on the playing-fields of Eton. Whether this was true or not, Dr Hahn contended that stamina had been a vital factor in destroying German military might in Europe. In a sense Hahn was a German disciple of Dr Thomas Arnold of Rugby, whose principles, he freely admitted, he absorbed and endorsed.

Hahn's first insight into English teaching occurred while he was studying at Oxford University as a Rhodes Scholar in the pre-First World War period. Later, during his years at Salem, he was criticized for attempting to Anglicize German education. This was not entirely true. His desire to develop physique and the intellect, applying both in the service of society, was derived from the ancient Greeks; he drew considerably from Plato's *Republic*. In Sparta the hierarchy had arranged for their sons to live and study together in groups from the age of seven, each group supervised by a master with a prefect as leader. (Similarly, at Gordonstoun a master, assisted by a head boy, would be in charge of each house.) In these select communities training was rigorous and often harsh, but it created amazing standards of endurance. Spartanism as encouraged by Dr Hahn, however, was less demanding, his objective being to stimulate in his pupils powers of self-discipline, pitting their skill against the elements both on land and at sea.

At Salem scholars were chosen exclusively from the upper stratum of German society, but before being accepted each candidate had first to undergo Hahn's close scrutiny as regards their character, intellect and knowledge. In the process of selection a boy's academic skills were in no way the guiding factor. Obviously such skills were desirable, but the Hahn system aimed primarily not at lofty academic skill but at fostering an adventurous spirit and physical endurance in manly activities; in short, to foster self-reliance and self-control. Thus such pursuits as mountaineering, sailing, athletics and rigorous expeditions ranked as highly as the normal school curriculum.

The time was approaching when Dr Hahn himself would need all the endurance he could muster. As a Jew he had openly opposed the rise of Nazism, and he was arrested in 1933 when Adolf Hitler came to power. On his release Kurt Hahn fled from persecution, leaving Germany for ever to start afresh in Britain, the country he admired so much. Circumstances now presented him with a challenge. Nazism had also annihilated the Salem experiment, but he was determined that it should not die. The rugged grandeur of Morayshire had fascinated him on walks during vacations at Oxford. It was there that he took the remnants of his tattered school. Luckily people with influence rallied to his aid, among them Mr C. E. Elliott, the headmaster of Eton, John Buchan (later Lord Tweedsmuir), the author, Dr William Temple, Archbishop of Canterbury, Admiral Sir Herbert Richmond and Professor G. M. Trevelyan, the historian. With their support he leased turreted Gordonstoun and three hundred heather-clad acres overlooking the Moray Firth.

Ironically the estate was then the property of the Gordon-Cummings family, whose ancestor, Sir William, the fourteenth baronet, had been concerned in the baccarat scandal in 1890. An earlier Prince of Wales, Prince Charles's great-great-grandfather, had dealt the cards at Sir William's Tranby Croft estate and in the legal action that ensued Gordon-Cummings had been accused of cheating. That was not the sum total of the notorious past of Gordonstoun's owners. On one side of the attractive mansion, with its pepper-pot turrets and balustraded roof, stands the Round Square, a circular

Prince Charles and .
Princess Anne, Malta,
1954. (*Keystone*)

Investiture,
Caernarvon, 1969.
(*Keystone*)

Prince Charles and
Prince Edward,
Buckingham Palace.
(*Keystone*)

Prince Charles
presenting the 1970
Carl Alan Award to
Jimmy Saville and the
pop group 'The
Tremeloes'. (*Keystone*)

Prince Charles given Freedom of the City of London : with the Lady Mayoress, Lady Studd, at the Guildhall. (*Syndication International*)

Prince Charles and Princess Anne on safari at Keekorok, Kenya, 1971. (*Syndication International*)

Prince Charles at Balmoral with his cousin Lady Sarah, aged 8. (*Camera Press*)

HRH Prince Charles and Prince Philip. (*Camera Press*)

Prince Charles visits the Community Relations Commission in London. (*Syndication International*)

Prince Charles presents prizes at Driving Society Show at Smith's Lawn, Windsor. (*Syndication International*)

Bowman Prince.
(*Camera Press*)

Royal encounter.
(*Camera Press*)

Prince Charles during his Canadian visit. (*Camera Press*)

Prince Charles in Indian head dress, Canada, 1977. (*Rex Features*)

Prince Charles on the West African tour in 1977, inspecting soldiers on parade. (*Rex Features*)

Prince Charles in polo gear. (*Rex Features*)

lawn hemmed in by the stable quarter. Here, many years ago, the laird of the day was said to be in communion with the Devil. Nowadays it caters for a dual purpose: it is both one of the school houses and an open-air theatre. Nearby is one of four pigeon-cotes that that same laird had constructed, labouring under the misguided belief that to keep pigeons was to guarantee the death of one's wife.

In the summer of 1934 Dr Hahn resurrected his school, this time amid the pines and Sitka spruce of Scotland. With him were three pupils – one of whom was Prince Philip – and a smattering of masters, including Mr Robert Chew, a Cambridge graduate who had taught mathematics for four years at Salem. Now he also supervised climbing and sailing and became Prince Philip's housemaster, the 'house' being a group of huts christened Windmill Lodge. These were erected near a derelict mill, which was itself destined to be renovated and converted into the masters' residence.

Some hundreds of years earlier the Cistercians had thrived at Salem, administering to the needs of the vicinity. This altruism was revived by Hahn and his pupils, to whom teaching of the Scriptures was an essential study. This tradition was entrenched from the outset in the Gordonstoun curriculum. To the heir apparent this was a decided advantage. He was intrigued by the tenets of the Christian faith, not merely because one day he would be the secular head of the Anglican Church but because the Scriptures held intrinsic interest for him. In spite of the prevailing drift away from religion, the young Prince, reared in a truly Christian environment, was more acquainted with the Bible than most of his fellows.

During the Second World War the school was evacuated from Gordonstoun, which was almost demolished by flames when it was occupied by troops. Hahn took his pupils to Wales, to Llandinan, a lovely village in Montgomeryshire. On the coast, some thirty miles away, lay Aberdovey, and it was there that Kurt Hahn founded his first Outward Bound School, where his character-moulding technique was compressed into one-month courses.

By the time Charles went to reside at Gordonstoun five similar schools would be flourishing in Britain, with counterparts in Australia, The Netherlands, Germany, Malaya and Rhodesia. Hahn's influence was spreading abroad. Appropriately, bearing in mind the inspiration of Plato's moral philosophy, a Greek system approximating to Hahn's had been set up at Arravryta not far from Athens. There were also the Atlantic Colleges, the first of which appeared in

Glamorgan, at St Donat's Castle, once the Welsh home of the American newspaper magnate, Mr William Randolph Hearst.

At Gordonstoun there was a shift in the main objective of Dr Hahn's educational system. Now in close proximity to Britain's independent schools, he claimed to see a flaw in their structure. 'I estimated,' he said, 'that about sixty per cent of boys have their vitality damaged under the conditions of modern boarding schools.' As a balancing tactic he proposed 'to kindle on the threshold of puberty non-poisonous passions which act as guardians during the dangerous years'.

There were cynics who now insinuated that Dr Hahn was endeavouring to Germanize education, but it would be difficult to fathom their reasoning when the basic conception was simply the building up of self-reliance and public service. The latter is applied in four ways: the fire unit, trained by expert members of the National Fire Service, and a recognized auxiliary in its own right; assistance at a coastguard station, which, fitted with rockets and life-saving equipment, maintains a look-out in foul weather for vessels in distress; a mountain rescue unit; and a team qualified to save swimmers in difficulty.

The school motto, *Plus est en vous* ('There is more in you') – inspiring boys to stretch their physical and mental capacities to their fullest extent – crystallized concisely the spirit of this unusual establishment. Two years after Gordonstoun's inception, Kurt Hahn collaborated with Elgin Academy to introduce the Moray Badge, from which the County Badge scheme emerged. It is not difficult to appreciate what inspired the Duke of Edinburgh to found his award scheme years later.

Having one more term to complete at Cheam, Prince Charles returned there after the Christmas holidays in 1961. Already the cynics were insinuating that the choice of Gordonstoun had been imperative because of the Prince's inability to pass the common-entrance examination to any other school. It so happens that Gordonstoun sets no proficiency test. Despite Mr Beck's assurances that the Prince could have entered most senior independent schools on merit, the Queen insisted that he should sit a normal proficiency examination to be set by the Gordonstoun staff. Charles, who had recently undergone an operation for appendicitis, passed and entered Gordonstoun entirely by personal effort and not because he was heir to the throne.

Unknown to the press, Mr Chew, who had succeeded Dr Hahn on the latter's retirement, visited Cheam that term to question Mr Beck on the royal pupil. To discourage the media from concentrating unreasonably on the activities of Prince Charles, the Queen's Press Secretary had issued this letter a few days earlier:

'When publicity was reduced at the end of the first term at Cheam School, it became possible for the whole school to function in the normal way and therefore the Prince of Wales was able to receive a normal education . . . For this the Queen and the Duke of Edinburgh are grateful, and I am asked to say that they hope that this happy state of affairs may continue during the Prince's stay at Gordonstoun. Her Majesty and His Royal Highness fully understand the very natural interest in the Prince of Wales's education, but they feel that he will only be able to derive full benefit from his days at school if he is not made the centre of special attention.'

The Prince of Wales was thirteen and a half when he joined about sixty other pupils at Windmill Lodge, a low structure of stone and wood, with a green asbestos roof, standing about a quarter of a mile from the main building. As he took a cold shower on the morning of his first day at Gordonstoun, the young Prince must have felt extremely lonely, and maybe rather distressed, knowing that he was the object of curiosity of all in school. The qualms he had first experienced at Cheam shrank to insignificance beside the mental pain he now endured. His shy, sensitive nature reacted unfavourably to the austerities of the dormitory: walls deliberately starved of paint, the bleakness of the wooden floorboards, the severity intensified by the naked electric light bulbs dangling from a cheerless ceiling. Other than the iron beds (only the head boy slept on an easy mattress), furniture was notably absent. Clothes were stored away in locker rooms and for study there were huts near by. At mealtimes Prince Charles went to Gordonstoun House, sharing a table with thirteen companions.

Gordonstoun was the complete answer to those who had wrongly accused the royal family of pandering to privilege. By the time the Prince of Wales arrived there, the school had ceased to be a prerogative of the rich. Now, in keeping with democratic times, enrolment was based on the qualities of the boy himself and not on his family's social status. Maximum fees in 1962 totalled £519, but fees were assessed according to parents' income. Thus the wealthy were expected to subsidize others of more modest means. Indeed the Prince's own house formed a microcosm of current society: for instance whereas the head boy or 'Foreman' (a function that the Prince's father had himself fulfilled), was the eighteen-year-old son of a Ross businessman, there was also a fisherman's son from Banff, an Edinburgh lawyer's son, a farmer's boy from Aberdeenshire and the two sons of a Lossiemouth general medical practitioner.

The Hahn philosophy had changed, concerning itself not with class but with countering the decay in the texture of modern society. In a sense his pupils, irrespective of social background, were intended to be his disciples in an attempt to stem the decline. Quite rightly Hahn was worried by the widespread deterioration of self-discipline, spurred on by such insidious practices as drug-taking; by the decay of physical fitness arising from an excess of mechanical mobility rather than dependence on one's own physical efforts; and by the decline in enterprise, which has become the victim of what Hahn described as 'spectatoritis' instead of personal participation. Then there was the increasing lack of enthusiasm for competence in human skills; and, finally, the depressing apathy to the suffering of others, stimulated by such factors as excessive violence – so often eulogized – on television and cinema screens. Training at Gordonstoun was therefore directed just as much to character building as it was to developing academic talent.

Service to the community was imprinted on the Prince's young mind from the beginning. Instead of the fagging system, he and other juniors shared the chores that are essential to the smooth running of communal life. Charles took his turn waiting on his classmates at table, tidying up the form-room, waking the rest of the boys of the house in the morning at a quarter to seven and weeding the garden. In his first term, emptying the dustbin, he noted, seemed to occur far more frequently for him than for his contemporaries. To the ex-monitor and captain of the first football eleven at Cheam, these menial tasks seemed not so much an indignity but merely another irksome aspect of Gordonstoun. Like the rest of the scholars, he cleaned his own shoes and made his own bed. For a while, finding it difficult to adjust to his new surroundings, he tried to leave, in vain requesting the Queen Mother to intercede and secure his parents' agreement.

*

Irrespective of the time of year, on being awakened the boys, dressed in shorts and running shoes, ran round the grounds or participated in physical drill, followed by a wash and cold shower. After that the following programme was to be the Prince's daily routine for the next four years:

8.15 a.m.	breakfast and surgery (when necessary)
8.55 a.m.	morning prayers
9.10 a.m.	classwork – five forty-minute periods including running, jumping, discus-throwing and javelin-throwing under the supervision of the physical training master
1.20 p.m.	lunch – followed by a twenty-minute rest period when music was played or someone read aloud to the boys relaxing on their backs
2.30 p.m.	afternoon activities:
	3 days a week either games (rugger and hockey in winter; cricket, lawn tennis or athletics in summer), seamanship or practical work on the estate
	1 day a week allocated to the Services: Coastguard Watchers, Army Cadets, Scouts, Fire Service, Mountain Rescue and Surf Life-Saving
	1 afternoon and evening individual projects – which were exhibited and judged at the end of each year
	every Saturday afternoon matches and opportunities for expeditions
4.00 p.m.	warm wash and cold shower
	change into evening school uniform
	tea, followed by two classes or tutorial periods
6.20 p.m.	supper, followed by preparation in the houses or by 'societies'
9.15 p.m.	bedtime, with a silence period of five minutes
9.30 p.m.	lights out

Charles chose for his manual work such activities as fence-repairing, brick-laying or cutting logs on the estate. Although he was ready to participate, he never approached team games with enthusiasm. This did not matter, since the sea intrigued him more and at Gordonstoun mastery of the sea was thought to be much more laudable; the tiny harbour of Hopeman, about two miles away, was held to be the school's 'best playing-field'. Initiative tests such as a canoe expedition from Hopeman Beach to Findhorn Bay and back (a voyage of more than twenty-four miles in rough sea) and exploratory hikes of some fifty miles contributed to his qualifying to Junior Training Plan after his first year.

In his first term he had shown his mettle, winning his 'greys' – that is, he replaced his grey shorts with navy blue shorts and sweater – and had ended 'very near the top of his form'. 'The Prince', revealed his report, 'joins in everything and has no special privileges. His parents will have to decide in the next eight weeks whether he will take languages when he goes into the Upper Fourth. He may try a combination of the two, science and languages. He may do mathematics and physics and still French and German.'

The autumn term came and went. Charles's beloved Highlands cast off their golden hues and donned the morose livery of winter. Christmas was spent with the royal family at Sandringham, then Charles flew to Bavaria, visiting an uncle, Prince Georg Wilhelm of Hanover, and his aunt, Princess Sophie, one of Prince Philip's three sisters, before learning to ski in the Engadine. When on a previous occasion he had visited all his German relations, Prince Philip had piloted the plane. But this time Charles travelled alone.

Staying overnight at Prince Georg's villa at Neuhaus, he was driven to the Swiss mountain resort of Tarasp, some four thousand feet up the Engadine, to Haus Muntanetz, the home of Prince Ludwig of Hesse, a cousin of Prince Philip. This was to be the setting for Charles's initial confrontation with the European press. No sooner did he appear with his instructor, Gisep Heinrich, than scores of reporters, photographers and sightseers swooped.

'His Royal Highness [wrote one Swiss correspondent] had reckoned without the inborn stubbornness of the pressmen, and they without the powdery snow, beautiful for skiing but not for hot-footing after skiers, especially in the thin city shoes most of them still wore. Before long most of them were floundering waist-deep, trying vainly to prevent snow being scooped up by the deep barrels of their long telephoto lenses. All became victims of the treacherous surface after only a few eager steps. Some went down gallantly. Some went down cursing. But all got up again – and again and again.'

Princess Margaret of Hesse pleaded with the crowd to refrain from obstructing the Prince further. 'He has only eight days in which to learn to ski and have some fun at it,' she pleaded. But in vain; everyone behaved with frenetic tenacity, like bees locating honey.

In the end Charles had no alternative but to retreat with Heinrich for instruction in the grounds of the Haus Muntanetz. Not until the following Sunday did the photographers, both professional and amateur, have the chance to resume their capers. When Charles embarked on a two-hour sleigh ride they 'waited at the first corner with their shutters cocked'. Raising his own camera, he focused on the photographers, who, momentarily outwitted, followed in pursuit 'in a long convoy of cars bearing half a dozen different national number-plates. It was like a snow scene from a Keystone Kops movie ... as they [the cars] leaped, slithered and bumped into each other in a frantic race for the best positions behind the speeding sleighs.' There were shouts in English, Italian, German and French as the wheels spun and skidded in a crazy stampede to catch the fleeing Prince.

This encounter with the press had filled the Prince of Wales with a mixture of annoyance and amusement, but later that year another incident would rouse his anger. His progress in seamanship had qualified him for a place in the crew of the *Pinta*, a Bermuda-rigged yacht, one of the vessels owned by Gordonstoun and used in maritime tests. Engaged on a cruise to the Outer Hebrides, the *Pinta* entered Stornoway harbour on the Isle of Lewis on a day in June. The yacht and her billowing canvas had long been familiar to the islanders, some of whom now hurried to the anchorage to see if Prince Charles was aboard. With four other boys, the Prince had been granted leave to have lunch ashore, then visit a cinema. But as they strolled to the Crown Hotel, accompanied by Donald Green, the Prince's private detective, the young heir apparent was quickly recognized, and to his embarrassment a crowd soon grew.

After that it is difficult to dissociate fact from fiction. While Green hurried off to book seats at the cinema, Charles, who had been left in the lounge, was later seen in the bar. One version purports that, no longer able to tolerate being stared at, he escaped to a neighbouring room, only to find that he was in the bar. Again there were the peering faces and the confused Prince, knowing that he must buy a drink or leave, asked for what he had once been given when shooting at Sandringham — a cherry brandy. Charles paid his half-crown and innocently raised a ridiculous storm in a liqueur glass. At that moment in walked 'that dreadful woman', a freelance journalist who set off a chain-reaction of publicity that flashed round the world.

It has also been implied that the Prince foolishly bought the drink because he 'may have been led into the prank'. Whatever the cause, the resultant uproar was grossly out of proportion to the alleged offence. The simple facts are these. Whatever the circumstances, Prince Charles was fourteen and had broken the law, for the Licensing (Scotland) Act of 1959 forbids anyone under eighteen to buy or consume excisable liquor on licensed premises. If he had been sixteen or more he could have ordered beer, cider, perry or porter. What was unreasonable and certainly hypocritical was that on these periodic visits, Gordonstoun pupils had usually ordered a glass of some alcoholic drink – a habit that all concerned had overlooked. Clearly if it had been any boy other than Prince Charles, the matter would have been ignored. Instead the incident grew to such magnitude that one questions the sanity of all concerned. One derived the impression that the Prince had been engaged in a drunken orgy. Throughout Britain the devotees of total abstinence threw up their arms in horror: teenage decadence had even caught up with the heir to the throne!

The incident cropped up at an unfortunate time, for the Prince had already had to suffer the contumely of others. In the previous September the League Against Cruel Sports, in conference in London's Caxton Hall, had publicly reproached Prince Charles for having shot his first stag on the Balmoral estate. And during March a minister of the Free Church of Scotland had rebuked him for skiing on the sabbath in the Cairngorms with other Gordonstoun pupils. Three months later, in May, a stricture had also been voiced in the House of Commons: in Standing Committee, while debating a bill for the protection of deer, someone had focused attention on 'the Duke of Edinburgh, who goes in for this loathsome kind of sport and even brings his child up to do it'.

What exacerbated matters in the Stornoway incident was an official denial from Buckingham Palace. Again, two different causes have been put forward. One claims that confusion arose over the subsequent telephone conversation with the Prince's detective. The other attributes the error to Mr Green's efforts to shield the Prince, believing that, in the circumstances, it was the wiser course. Whatever the true reason, the outcome was the same: rather humiliatingly, the denial was withdrawn and Scotland Yard was instructed to probe its origin.

Police proceedings against the hotelier were announced, then withdrawn, but unfortunately similar leniency was withheld from Charles. When the *Pinta* moored again on the mainland and the Prince of Wales returned to Gordonstoun, he mounted the impressive wooden staircase to the headmaster's study overlooking ornamental water and chestnut trees. Innocently or foolishly, Charles had committed a breach of the Gordonstoun code. Some days later Mr Chew announced that the incident was closed. As for the Prince, he escaped a caning, but to his dismay his Junior Training Plan was withdrawn and he had to begin again from scratch. It was disheartening, but by the end of the term he had regained his status. From then onwards he would attain every grade of Gordonstoun's unique pattern of promotion, graduating to Senior Training Plan, White Stripe and Colour Bearer Candidate. Above these came the pupils' hierarchy : the captains and their assistants, and over them that exalted being, the Guardian – a distinction that the Prince would achieve, as his father had before him.

If nothing else as yet had pinpointed the care with which he, as heir apparent, must conduct himself, the Stornoway incident had. It had, moreover, a more incisive impact on his sensitivity than was generally thought. Figuratively, for a long time his treatment from the press would fester.

However, a further incident in September 1964 would afford him a measure of satisfaction. With Prince Philip and Princess Anne, the Prince of Wales attended the wedding in Greece of King Constantine of the Hellenes to Princess Anne-Marie of Denmark. It was also an opportunity to sunbathe with the Swedish Crown Prince Gustaf and other young guests at Vouliagmeni near Athens. Greek naval police patrolled to ward off press intruders, but three photographers eluded them, boarding Prince Charles's raft. As was later angrily explained in French newspapers, two of the trespassers were summarily doused in the sea. This brusque treatment was attributed to the British and Swedish Princes, but it was Charles's German cousins who reached them first.

Adverse publicity erupted again when the Prince returned to the peace and loneliness of his Highland school. Like the other pupils, for some time he had been required to write a weekly essay on varied topics; these had accumulated to fill eight exercise books. Now, unknown to him, one had vanished.

Past experience had indicated that a high value was placed on any item bearing the Prince's name and house. Already one exercise book had been hawked for sale until it was proved without doubt to be a forgery. A second book, thrown into a wastepaper basket by one of the masters, had eventually been recognized as that of someone else. But now it was the authentic article, an olive-green exercise book, that was missing and the contents were indisputably in the Prince's own handwriting.

Regrettably Charles was unaware of his book's disappearance until some of the essays appeared during November in the German magazine *Stern*. Meanwhile Scotland Yard traced the original manuscript to an office in St Helens in Lancashire. In the same month the local Mercury Press issued a writ against the Metropolitan Police, seeking its return. Photostat copies, it was learnt, had been offered for sale to the British and foreign press and it was one of these that had eventually reached Hamburg, to be published under the misleading headline – 'The Confessions of Prince Charles'. The royal pupil's neat handwriting confirmed without doubt that the stolen book was by no means spurious.

One essay, falsely presented as conveying the Prince's opinions of power and its corrupting influences, was in fact nothing more than a condensation of extracts from Lecky's *History of England*. Three other essays, however, did give an insight into the Prince's views. In one – based on democracy and the operation of the principle of one man, one vote – he was 'troubled by the fact that voters today tended to go for a particular party and not for the individual candidate, because they vote for the politics of a party,' revealed the Bonn correspondent of *The Times*. The Prince also queried the wisdom of giving a vote to an unattractive Tory candidate 'because the elector is opposed to the nationalisation of steel or abolishing public schools'. Because of the Stornoway affair in particular, the second essay – on radio, television and the press – might have been steeped in sourness, yet he upheld their right to the freedom to 'protect people from the government in many ways, by letting them know what is going on, maybe behind their backs in some cases'. He also commended the value of television for stimulating the minds of the young. In the third essay (for which he had been given ten minutes to complete), Charles was asked to name the four articles he would take with him should a nuclear crisis force him to seek refuge on a remote island. He chose a tent, a knife, 'lots of rope and string' and a small radio to receive news and communicate if possible with the outside world. He visualized, however, that in the event of anything so calamitous, most people, 'including me, would get into a frightful panic'.

The dubious manner in which these essays had been secured prompted the comment from Buckingham Palace that it was 'highly regrettable that the private essays of a schoolboy should have been published at all in this way'. As if to deliberately antagonize them, *Stern* now published sketches of 'Papa' and 'Mama', the work, it was claimed, of Charles when four years old.

But what incensed the royal family was the contemptible allegation that the Prince, sorely in need of pocket money, had sold his essays to a fellow pupil for thirty shillings. In an article entitled 'The Princely Pauper', the American magazine *Time* claimed to outline the disreputable circumstances by which the essays had appeared in *Stern*. In mentioning that Charles had parted with his book for financial gain, they made the second despicable implication that he had offered his autograph for sale at Cheam. If *Time* was accurate, the Hamburg magazine had paid £1,000 for Charles's schoolboy writings; an additional £4,000, it was claimed, was realized from other transactions.

It is exceedingly rare for the royal family either to confirm or to deny comment, yet the Queen's Press Secretary wrote to *Time*:

'There is no truth whatever in the story that Prince Charles has sold his autograph at any time. There is also no truth whatever that he sold his composition book to a classmate. In the first place he is intelligent and old enough to realise how embarrassing this would turn out to be, and second he is only too conscious of the interest of the Press in anything to do with himself and his family. The suggestion that his parents keep him short of money, that he has to find other means to raise it, is also a complete invention. Finally, the police would not have attempted to regain the composition book unless they were quite satisfied that it had been obtained legally.'

To the rational mind it is puzzling that newspaper and magazine editors on the Continent and in the United States should seize on any scrap of news, true or false, concerning the royal family. They do so with an avidity that seems psychopathic. When in 1958 Commander Colville protested on behalf of the Queen at the spate of inaccurate and foolish publicity given by the press, it was a genuine grievance. According to Kingsley Martin in *The Crown and the Establishment*,

'... at one time American magazines kept permanent correspondents in

England with the job of prying into the private affairs of the royal family and ... the police knew of as many as thirty men and women who earned their living by buying and selling "Palace secrets". In November 1959 Mr. George Murray, the acting chairman of the Press Council, speaking in Bonn to an audience of journalists and parliamentarians, said that ... the Queen and her family were entitled to their privacy, and there were limits of tolerance on Press publicity.'

The Scandinavian and the Dutch royal households are never subjected to the sort of treatment meted out to Prince Charles and Princess Anne when they visited Liechtenstein after Christmas as the guests of Prince Franz Josef and his wife, Princess Gina, for winter sports. The continental photographers again clung like leeches. Finally a compromise was reached whereby the photographers were allowed to take photographs in the afternoon, provided the Prince and Princess could have their mornings free from interference.

On his return to Gordonstoun the year 1965 proved to be the most congenial period in the Prince's school life. He now had the privacy of his own study and his attendance at St Paul's Cathedral for the state funeral of Sir Winston Churchill was the only public ceremony allowed to interfere with his studies. Under the Gordonstoun system, the tempo of self-discipline had been speeded up. Team games were still played, though more out of a sense of duty. He still derived genuine enjoyment from field sports. Polo was now included among his outdoor passions. Indoors his addiction to the arts was allowed unstinted scope.

He was also drawn to the theatre – comedy as well as drama. Whereas nature never invested the son with the father's wit, one can say with equal conviction that Prince Philip is not endowed with humour like his son's. Prince Charles is attracted by the Goon variety of comedy. It was not comedy but high drama that he portrayed on the night of 27 November 1965, when he played the title role in Shakespeare's *Macbeth*. To Charles the story of this immortal tragedy had long been indelibly printed on his mind, for tradition asserts that it was Glamis Castle, the ancestral home of the Queen Mother, that was the medieval setting for this gruesome tale. The Prince of Wales found depicting the character of Macbeth, with its contrasting aspects of good and evil, more rewarding than distinction in mathematics; it involved probing what was fast becoming an engrossing subject – the behaviour and history of man. Of his performance, the *Gordonstoun Record* commented that he was 'at his very best in the quiet poetic soliloquies, the poetry of which he so beautifully brought out and in the bits which expressed Macbeth's terrible agony of remorse and fear. In the second part of the play, he equally well expressed the degenerative hardening of Macbeth's character, the assumption of cynicism in an attempt to blunt the underlying and too painful moral sensitivity.'

For a while, however, the Prince was to leave his school in the Highlands; there would be an interlude of six months in Australia before he completed his studies at Gordonstoun.

4 Timbertop and Trinity

For some while the royal family had pondered how to extend the Prince's horizons to the wider world of the Commonwealth. While attending the Commonwealth Conference during the previous summer, Sir Robert Menzies, the Australian Prime Minister, on being invited to Balmoral by the Queen and Prince Philip, had advised them that Prince Charles should enter the exclusive Geelong Church of England Grammar School in Victoria. His choice was confirmed by others, among them the Archbishop of Melbourne, brother of the Dean of Windsor, and Sir Alexander Downer, the High Commissioner for Australia.

Thus on 19 November 1965 it was officially announced that Charles and an Australian boy – whose identity was later disclosed as that of David Manton, a wealthy sheep-farmer's son – should exchange schools for one term (although this was later extended to two). The Prince of Wales was not, however, to reside at the main establishment near Melbourne but at Timbertop, Geelong's unconventional offshoot, about one hundred miles to the north on the fringe of the timbered slopes of Mount Buller.

Australians generally welcomed the announcement: not for forty-five years had a Prince of Wales set foot in their country. But as in the case of Cheam and Gordonstoun, the decision spontaneously provoked a clash of views. In a controversial exchange, a Labour member in the Canberra Parliament demanded to know why Sir Robert had been so undemocratic; there were many admirable state high schools from which to choose. The Prime Minister replied that at Balmoral he had been asked for advice.

'I was quite detached, personally, because I went to another school, which, presumably, from the honourable member's question, isn't so exclusive or toney. Geelong Grammar is a school of high repute and it is not difficult for people to understand that a school that has a rural branch has attractions in this instance. I would be very sorry for the young Prince if he were at school in the middle of a crowded city in Australia with people gazing at him, with people trying to get pictures of him, and with people making him a raree show. That isn't what he will be there for. He will be here to go to school and mix with ordinary Australian boys.'

Others entered the verbal fray. Voicing the opinion of the Australian Parents' and Citizens' Association, a representative claimed that Timbertop was no more typical of Australia than Gordonstoun was typical of Britain, while the New South Wales Teachers' Federation argued that if the idea was 'for Prince Charles to meet Australians, then he should meet ordinary Aussies. Geelong caters for the sons of wealthy families.' Even critics in Britain contributed their strictures, and although it was no concern of America, the *New York Herald Tribune* dismissed Timbertop as just another 'of those curious schools where the bleakness of life is in direct ratio to cost of tuition'.

But whether it was a state or private school was immaterial. Of far greater significance was the fact that Prince Charles was being sent to the antipodes – an act that, as Sir Robert Menzies commented, was 'a very tangible demonstration of the close ties between Australia and the Royal Family. The idea of the young Prince of Wales living and studying here in his formative years is a prospect that will give widespread satisfaction. It is an imaginative and practical step. Getting to know Australia through young Australians should prove of inestimable value for a prince whose future duties will require a comprehensive knowledge of the countries and peoples of the Commonwealth.'

Geelong Grammar School originated in 1857, the creation of an Anglican Bishop of Melbourne, but Timbertop was of more recent foundation, begun by a former headmaster, Dr Darling, after the Second World War. Previously he had taught at Charterhouse School in Surrey, and had been intrigued by Dr Hahn's ideals. Unable to apply them at Geelong itself, he had set up his colony amid the picturesque loneliness of the Victorian outback. Since then more than a hundred pupils had moved from Geelong to the austerities of Timbertop for their fourth year, living in eight huts, with fifteen boys in each.

It was the end of January 1966 when Prince Charles flew from Heathrow airport for Australia. Similar misgivings to those that had overtaken him the day he left Balmoral for Cheam now returned.

He was travelling to the other side of the world, not merely as a schoolboy but as a future King of Australia (assuming that republicanism allowed it by the time he wore the crown). Therefore much more was at stake than education. In Australia he would be subjected to the most stringent examination, an unenviable ordeal for a shy – even blushing – seventeen-year-old, who contemplated the months ahead with trepidation. Even more disconcerting was the fact that, for the first time, he was being pushed into the royal limelight on his own. No longer was there any senior member of the royal family to shield him from some of the glare. Whether he was a failure or a success would depend now entirely on his own initiative.

As he has grown older, the Prince has exhibited traits that cast him in much the same mould as his great-grandfather and grandfather, George v and George vi. Both suffered from a surfeit of introspection, anxiously expecting the worst in situations that they had never previously experienced. When they realized that their fears were baseless, they expressed their astonishment with almost childish delight. When, for instance, George v and Queen Mary toured the East End of London during their Silver Jubilee celebration in May 1935, the King was so moved by the outburst of public affection that he remarked with naïveté to the Archbishop of Canterbury: 'I had no idea they felt like that about me. I am beginning to think that they must really like me for myself.'

Prince Charles need have had no fears. He would eventually assess his Australian stay as 'the most wonderful period of my life'. Although to many in the western world the Australians appear to be rather crude in speech and behaviour, the Prince – after the initial abrupt impact – grew to adore them. They in their turn generously bestowed on him such native endearments as 'Good on yer, Pommy bastard'.

At the Timbertop estate, which covered some twenty thousand acres of bush country at about two thousand feet above sea-level, a former member of the Metropolitan Police, Detective Inspector Derek Sharp, safeguarded the royal student, while Squadron Leader David Checketts, an equerry of Prince Philip, rented a farm for himself and his family some 120 miles from the colony and attended to any public matters affecting the Prince. Charles sometimes lived on the farm at weekends. But the Prince needed no protection – not even from what was usually the immoderate preoccupation of the press. Quite sensibly an agreement was arrived at whereby the Australian press was empowered to produce all the information and photographs it needed during Charles's first day at the colony. After that no one was to interfere with the school's usual routine.

How Charles reacted to his new life can best be ascertained from his own words – an article that was published in the *Gordonstoun Record* under the title: 'Timbertop, or Beating about the Bush'.

'A popular cry [he wrote] seems to be that Timbertop is very similar to Gordonstoun. This is not strictly true ... From what I make of it, Timbertop is very individual. All the boys are virtually the same age, 14–15; there are no prefects and the masters do all the work that boys might otherwise do in a school. This way I think there is much more contact between masters and boys as everyone is placed in the same sort of situation. Almost everyone, masters and boys, enjoy themselves up here and don't look forward to the restrictions of the main school when they go back ... but ... there's very little [spare time] and one never seems to stop running here and there for one minute of the day, from 7-30 a.m. breakfast – and no morning run, though there's worse to follow – until the lights go out at 9-15 p.m., having had tea at the unearthly hour of 5-30 p.m. If you have just done a cross-country run at 4-45 p.m., and arrived back at 5-5 p.m., it's difficult to persuade your stomach to accept food!'

There was the strenuous chore of tree-felling and wood-chopping. This was

'... essential as the boys' boilers have to be stoked with logs and the kitchen uses a huge number. The first week I was here I was made to go out and chop up logs on a hillside in boiling hot weather. I could hardly see my hands for blisters after that! Each afternoon after classes, which end at 3 o'clock, there are jobs which are rather equivalent to P.W., but involve chopping and splitting wood, feeding the pigs, cleaning out fly-traps (which are revolting glass bowls seething with flies and very ancient meat), or picking up bits of paper round the School. After these jobs a cross-country· is usually required twice a week, along a path through the bush. When the weather is hot and there is a lot of dust it is very unpleasant, but I believe it makes you reasonably fit to go on expeditions over the week-end.'

As at Gordonstoun, expeditions were a significant feature, but at Timbertop they occurred every weekend. 'After a puff up Mount Timbertop, which rises above the School, on the first Sunday, there were three more compulsory weekend expeditions to prepare one for going out for longer periods in the bush. All the mountains in the area are very thickly wooded, with equally thick undergrowth down below. When you are walking through the bush you can't see anything except gum-tree upon gum-tree, which tends to become rather monotonous . . .' One had to be careful when pitching camp

'. . . as a certain kind of gum-tree sheds its branches without warning. Apart from that you virtually have to inspect every inch of ground . . . in case there are any ants or other ghastly creatures. There is one species of ant called Bull Ants which are three-quarters of an inch long or more and they bite like mad!

'Some boys manage to walk fantastic distances over a week-end of four days or less, and do 130 or even 200 miles. The furthest I've been is 60–70 miles in three days, climbing about five peaks on the way. At the campsite the cooking is done on an open fire in a trench. You have to be very careful in hot weather that you don't start a bush fire, and at the beginning of this term there was a total fire ban in force, so that you ate all the tinned food cold.'

Somehow work was interspersed with these diversions. Obviously it could not be taken quite as seriously as in an ordinary school, 'but there are classes all morning after Chapel at 8.45 and there is a two-hour prep period in the evening'. Organized sports such as field games were totally absent,

. . . but each Wednesday there is either a tug o'war between the boys' units, or houses, or, if it's hot, there is swimming, or perhaps someone is feeling sufficiently cruel to organise a race that involves carrying half a tree for a certain distance. I almost convinced one or two Australians outside the school that we rustled kangaroos at Timbertop and that we performed this art by creeping up on them from behind, grabbing them by the tail and flicking them over on to their backs, where you had them at your mercy.

'The school is situated in the foothills of the Dividing Range and all the buildings are extraordinarily well hidden from view as there are gum-trees everywhere. The boys live in units, or bungalow-type buildings, of which there are nine, holding fifteen boys apiece. The Chapel is in the centre and is in the shape of a continuous steep roof that reaches to ground level. Behind the altar there is a huge window that looks out on to a series of ridges receding into the distance. When I arrived here everything was very dry and brown, but now it is all green since early rains came. I have been out to several farms in the area and have watched some shearing being done. I was asked to try my hand at it, but, of course, made rather a mess of it, and left a somewhat shredded sheep.

'Everyone asks how Australia compares with England, which is a very difficult question, as there isn't really a comparison. The mountains are so different from Scotland because of all the trees, and the countryside is so different from England because there are no ordered fields, but rolling hills covered in grass and with gum-trees dotted about everywhere. I came over here expecting boiling hot weather all the time, but one soon discovers one's error, and it can certainly become very cold, especially during winter, while it's the summer term at Gordonstoun.'

Activities at Timbertop by no means concentrated on manual work, attending to the pigs and chickens or taking one's turn as a 'slushy', or washer-up, in the kitchens, or pitting one's strength in tests of physical endurance. The Australian pupils were also engrossed in preparing for examinations and Prince Charles, who had the added responsibility of supervising fifteen schoolfellows, faced the prospect of A-level examinations in history and French the following year. He could not afford to fail. Although A-levels were not imperative for kingship, by some curious reckoning he was the only scholar in Britain whose school reports were laid bare to the cold light of international publicity.

At this phase of his scholastic career Charles was conducting his own studies. To the Prince, one of the gratifying aspects of Timbertop was the onus placed on his personal resources. Now and again he would consult a teacher at Geelong or submit an essay there, but his studies were not subjected to tutorial scrutiny until he went back to Scotland.

An event which left its indelible mark occurred towards the end of Charles's first term. At that time the headmaster at Geelong was Mr Thomas Garnett, formerly at Marlborough, who had himself studied at Charterhouse and Magdalen College, Cambridge. In keeping with a now accepted custom, he and a party of boys from Geelong and Timbertop made the periodic visit to missionary stations in New Guinea, the main overseas territory administered by the Australian Commonwealth. On the flight the aircraft touched down at Brisbane and Port Moresby and it was at the former – a refuelling station (where the news had been circulated that the Prince was on board) – that he emerged from his pupa of shyness. Today the Prince recalls the incident as a conclusive personal breakthrough. He confided to a friend that 'somebody on the 'plane said to me "Go on, go down and say hello to the crowd!" I looked out of the window at the terrifying sea of faces waiting for me on the tarmac, and I was so scared I could scarcely move. I had to be virtually kicked out of the 'plane, and as I walked towards the barriers, something clicked inside me. All my shyness suddenly disappeared – and really, from that moment on, I do not think I have ever felt nervous in public again.' This was the sign of a real monarch in the making.

The last stage of the journey was by water in the Anglican Mission launch across Goodenough Bay to Wedau near Dogura Cathedral. This was the sixth visit by Geelong pupils but it was notably different from the rest. This time there was the magnetic attraction of a Prince of the British royal household. Thousands of Australians and Papuans waited on a beach gilded by the setting sun. In this motley throng grass skirts and feathered head-dresses contrasted strikingly with the more precise uniforms of schoolchildren, nursing organizations and religious orders. On the jetty waited the church councillors, resplendent with red hibiscus. At first there was no ecstasy, no wild scrambling for a better view of the Prince; but the 'air was electric with excitement' as Dr John Chisholm, the bishop, officially welcomed the Prince. Suddenly there erupted a storm of shouting as the people cried *'Egualau!'*, which in Wedauan means 'Greeting!'.

In New Guinea Prince Charles experienced a rare sensation. As one writer has aptly put it, he witnessed scenes that recalled the Church in sixth-century England and in Scandinavia in the tenth and eleventh centuries: the Church administering to the educational, medical and charitable needs as well as the devotional requirements of the people. With almost one thousand communicants Charles attended Eucharist celebrated in the native tongue by the Papuan converts: an earnest expression of the people's unshakeable faith in the story of Christ, and a sight that the Prince would scarcely witness in an Anglican cathedral in twentieth-century Britain.

Like the other Geelong boys, the Prince of Wales recorded his impressions of New Guinea. 'I would like to mention,' he wrote, 'how fresh and sincere I found the Church at Dogura. Everyone was so eager to take part in the services, and the singing was almost deafening. One felt that it might almost be the original Church. Where Christianity is new, it must be much easier to enter into the whole spirit of it wholeheartedly, and it is rather wonderful that you can still go somewhere where this strikes you.'

Only in this Papuan fervour was it realized how considerably, in a materialistic Britain (in which Prince Charles would one day be called Defender of the Faith), support for the Church had ebbed. It seemed that there was little room for Christianity in modern civilization and this was stamped very forcibly on the Prince's mind. What he witnessed in New Guinea was the labour brought to fruition of those missionary pioneers, Albert Maclaren and Copland

King, in 1891. Yet one senses that the Prince, with an element of regret, feared that Papuan culture would change under western influence.

'I can't help feeling [he wrote] that less and less interest is being taken by the younger Papuans in the customs and skills of their parents and grandparents because they feel that they have to live up to European standards and that these things belong to the past and have no relevance to the present or future. This may be a completely false impression, but I was given one or two presents by young people and when I asked if they had made them, they said their mothers or aunts had. No doubt, however, in the years to come, when there are new generations of Papuans, they will consider these ancient skills of no use. But I expect there will be those to make souvenirs for tourists; or, if not, I hope a suitable amount of relics will be preserved for history.'

The half-year spent in Australia was so crammed with activity that the time seemed to pass phenomenally fast. The tough life of a lumberjack and such menial chores as floor-sweeping were remote from the opulence of Buckingham Palace. Years later he jocularly remarked that this phase of his life made him 'feel like an Outward Bound daily-help'. The work had not lacked variety. He had taken part in a scheme to aid Service widows, on one occasion helping to fell fifty-six tons of timber for the widows and their families in the nearby town of Mansfield. In the bush he had cooked his meals over camp fires like a jackaroo; had learnt the rudiments of gem-hunting in Glenrowan and of panning for gold; and at the Botanical Gardens in Canberra he had been instructed in the ornithological process called mist-netting. As Timbertop's most expert angler he had fished in the streams, and when the snow fell on their mountain setting he had trained his schoolmates to ski.

Prince Charles, like his parents, would never lay claim to being an intellectual, but his thirst for knowledge is unquenchable. His tour, accompanied by Squadron Leader Checketts, down the east coast of the continent, living with Australians at each stage, was embarked upon more as a quest for knowledge than as holiday relaxation. When he came to leave Australia in July, his headmaster could therefore report with justification that the Prince of Wales had 'met people of all ages ... Saw a good deal of eastern Australia and his visit to New Guinea made a deep impression on him.' Australians generally regretted that the 'Pommy bastard' was leaving them. Mr Garnett expressed it more euphemistically: 'Leaving aside the question of royalty, we have really enjoyed having Prince

Charles at the school. Before his visit most Australians had very hazy and possibly erroneous ideas of him, if they had any ideas at all. They probably thought of him as just a distant, uninteresting figurehead. In future most of them will know him as a friendly, intelligent, natural boy with a good sense of humour, someone who by no means has an easy task ahead of him in life.'

The regard was mutual. At the airport on the day of departure, the Prince, who left Timbertop with a presentation book containing the signatures of fellow-pupils, in his turn had a message for his future subjects.

'It would be difficult [read his equerry on his behalf] to leave without saying how much I have enjoyed and appreciated my stay in Australia and how touched I have been by the kindness of so many people making those six months such a worthwhile experience. The most wonderful part was the opportunity to travel and see ... some of the country (I hope I shall be able to come back and see the rest) and also the chance to meet so many people which completes the link with a country I am very sad to be leaving; and yet I shall now be able to visualise Australia in the most vivid terms, after such a marvellous visit.'

The real significance of Charles's period in Australia was that it brusquely shattered his acute diffidence. One recollects the nervous disposition of his grandfather, King George VI, and the manner in which it undermined him during years of kingship. Charles, who has inherited some of the late King's traits, might also have suffered similar hours of anguish. But today the Prince can reveal that, more than any other experience, his months in Australia 'opened my eyes. You are judged there on how people see you and feel about you. There are no assumptions. As a matter of fact, having a title, and being a member of the upper classes, as often as not militates against you in this country. In Australia you certainly have to fend for yourself. Australia got me over my shyness.'

From Australia the Prince and his equerry flew to Auckland, Tahiti and Mexico City, where he indulged his passion for the past by visiting the pyramids of Teotihuacan. From Mexico City he travelled to Jamaica, where Prince Philip and Princess Anne were attending the Commonwealth Games. Watching the athletes competing reminded Charles that he had been Prince of Wales for about eight years – since the day when, as a pupil at Cheam, the Queen had announced his creation at the Commonwealth Games in Cardiff. Since then he had attained to young manhood. To his great relief, his schooldays were coming to an end.

Returning to Gordonstoun in the autumn of 1966, he was installed as helper (or head) at Windmill Lodge and in the next, and final, term he rose to the honoured post of Guardian. Maybe at that time this elevation within the school hierarchy was paramount in his mind, rather than the fact that, now eighteen years old, he would be monarch in his own right, without the aid of a regent, if the Queen ceased to reign.

As head boy at Gordonstoun, the Prince of Wales was not empowered to punish, and he was more of an intermediary, linking the headmaster, housemasters and pupils together. In theory he had to ensure that all the pupils fulfilled their specific duties, but in practice the heads of houses and the custom of placing each individual on his honour simplified this responsibility. Briefly, he was the person who prepared and presented the pupils' petitions to the headmaster or appropriate housemaster. It was his privilege, too, to advise the rank and file and plead on their behalf, though his plea to cancel the expulsion of two boys proved quite abortive.

Meanwhile he was studying for his A-levels in history and French. He took the examinations in July 1967, and his success in both subjects was reported in the following September. Some years earlier he had been dismissed as rather a dull boy, the sceptics insinuating that only influence and prestige had gained him places at Cheam and Gordonstoun. Yet at Geelong his tutors unanimously agreed that his level of attainment would have guaranteed him entry to any Australian university. Now, in a report in *The Times* of 5 October 1967, Mr R. M. Todd, secretary of the Oxford and Cambridge Schools Examination Board, explained that the Prince of Wales excelled in his optional history paper – 'the one which marks out the "high flyers" as regards judgment, initiative, and historical acumen. If a boy has done well in this paper – and the Prince got a distinction – it is a very good guide to university.' He revealed, too, that of the total number of candidates – roughly four thousand – only slightly more than six per cent had gained distinctions in the special paper. 'I consider that his performance was extraordinary, especially when you consider that he was digging about in Australia and that kind of thing beforehand. He has so many things to do, he must have worked like a demon. I should hesitate to tackle the paper myself, it takes me back to the time when I did Greats.'

Mr Todd had referred to university. That would be the final stage of the Prince's education. Some weeks before he left Britain for Timbertop – on 22 December 1965 – five guests dined with the Queen and Prince Philip at Buckingham Palace. Between them these luminaries presented an amalgam of mature experience in markedly different spheres of life, since the group consisted of Dr Michael Ramsay, Archbishop of Canterbury; Dr Robert Woods, Dean of Windsor and the Queen's domestic chaplain; Mr Harold Wilson, the Prime Minister; Sir Charles Wilson, Principal of Glasgow University and currently chairman of the Committee of Vice-Chancellors; and Earl Mountbatten. They had assembled at the Queen's request to discuss and advise on a salient topic: the climax of Prince Charles's education when he left Gordonstoun. Although their paths had been widely divergent – leading to the Church, to politics, to the lecture-hall and the Navy – all five had been undergraduates as a prelude to their careers. The two Church dignitaries had graduated at Cambridge, the politician and the vice-chancellor at Oxford, and even the veteran sailor, who had graduated from the naval colleges at Osborne and Dartmouth to the rank of admiral, could reflect with delight on his university interlude: as a junior officer after the First World War, he had taken an abridged course at Christ's College, Cambridge.

In recent reigns, perhaps, Earl Mountbatten, whose Second World War adventures had fascinated Prince Charles, would have advocated the more traditional course for the heir apparent: Osborne, Dartmouth, then regular service, acquiring normal promotion and aspiring to a command. For years the heir apparent, whether he liked it or not, had been rigidly condemned to don the uniform of the Services and for a while to serve in one. Then royal personages had begun to appear, rather superficially, on the university scene. First Edward VII, as Prince of Wales, had attended three universities, but this had been more akin to academic sampling, for he remained strictly on the perimeter of undergraduate life. To some extent convention had been relaxed for Edward VIII and his brother, the future George VI, but much of the royal aloofness had refused to thaw. Times had changed at an astonishing tempo, however. That was why the Queen and Prince Philip had invoked others to contribute their wisdom and experience of Church, State and the academic world – institutions that affected the heir apparent in modern society. Apart from his normal duties in Glasgow, Sir Charles Wilson presided over the Committee of Vice-Chancellors, which, composed of Britain's foremost dons, tackled the problems springing from the growth of the new universities. Originating in Govan, Scotland, Sir Charles had lectured on 'Modern Greats' or PPE – philosophy, politics and economics – at Corpus Christi, Oxford. The Prime Minister, an elementary schoolboy in the Yorkshire wool town of Huddersfield, had gained the Gladstone Memorial Prize and a first-class degree, also in PPE, at Jesus College, Oxford.

Coming from people of such widely contrasting interests, the questions raised by this quintet of advisers at the December dinner party were varied and numerous. But it was not until a year later, when Prince Philip granted an interview to the court correspondent of the Press Association, that the gist of the deliberations was disclosed.

Prince Philip revealed that the choice of a university education was dictated by his son's own inclination. The Queen and himself had consistently described to Prince Charles what the situation and possibilities were and assured him that he himself was intrinsically involved in the choice of his education. Basically the alternative to a period at university was a spell in one of the Services. Because the Prince himself wanted to go to a university, 'we tried to figure out some way in which we could do this provided he was more or less qualified'. The dinner party, Prince Philip further revealed, played its part to this extent. Aware of what the Prince of Wales desired, his parents wished to ensure that the idea commended itself to these people – even if Charles was not entirely qualified – considering his almost inevitable future status as king. They also sought their guests' opinions as to the pattern of the programme the Prince should undertake: should he follow a regular university course and take a specific degree, or would it be more beneficial – in his unique position – if he were to devote time to a more generalized course with no degree in mind? 'It obviously entered into our minds that if he had spent part of his school education abroad in a Commonwealth country, whether perhaps the course ... should include a period in a Commonwealth university. This again would have made it more difficult to have pursued a specific subject.'

Discussion had also delved in a general way into the pros and cons of the new universities as opposed to the old :

'... the associations which they would have, the practical problems that they might raise, and so on ... As I see it now, there are three kinds of universities : there are the old universities ... the "red brick" universities, and the new universities. We discussed this at great length, and in the end we came to the conclusion that it is so difficult to choose between any of the new universities, and that particular associations which existed between one or another were so marginal that the consensus of opinion was that it should be one of the older ones. And Cambridge, I think, suggested itself for a number of reasons. His cousins had been there, his grandfather [too] ... and East Anglia is relatively close to Sandringham, and in a sense all reasonable arguments seemed to point to Cambridge.'

Prince Philip thought that his son would continue to read history :

'... we have not worked out what the course is to be. But we hope ... that it will include a number of fringe subjects ... which it will be valuable for him to have studied, rather than he should become an academic historian ... I think so many of the university programmes are geared to specialities, people ... who want to have a professional job. I think whatever he does there, it's more important ... that he should have a broad base of instruction ... I don't think the course should be constrained ... because of the absolute need to take a degree.'

Asked if the Prince might enter the Royal Navy after university, Prince Philip remarked : 'It would seem both natural and needful to him to have had some Service experience ... either by doing a longish experience in one Service or by doing attachments to all three ... it would be very useful to him in later life.'

Of one thing Prince Philip was certain : his son was looking forward to leaving school. 'There comes a moment when you have had enough of it.' But Charles would never regret his years at Gordonstoun, not because of its toughness

'... which [Prince Charles says] is too much exaggerated by report. It was the general character of the education there – Kurt Hahn's principles; an education which tried to balance the physical and mental with the emphasis on self-reliance to develop a rounded human being. I did not enjoy school as much as I might have, but that was because I am happier at home than anywhere else. But Gordonstoun developed my will-power and self-control, helped me to discipline myself, and I think that discipline, not in the sense of making you bath in cold water, but in the Latin sense – giving shape and form and tidiness to your life – is the most important thing your education can do.'

The scheme for Prince Charles to become an undergraduate had been finalized before he embarked for Australia. The question was: at which university? The choice would be his. A Scottish seat of learning was ruled out because he now wished to have a change of scene. His final decision was in keeping with his outlook and fundamental character. The Prince of Wales is fascinated by the past, an arresting trait in an heir apparent in an age when it is much more fashionable to decry it. He is no reactionary, but he feels profoundly the bond between himself and the past. To him tradition is not archaic but the solid basis of human foundation. Moreover, it is deep-rooted and therefore stable. There was also for him the appeal of ancient architecture, mellowed over the centuries. He reasoned that only Cambridge or Oxford essentially fitted into this general category, and by the time he had returned from Timbertop he had chosen Cambridge.

At the Queen's request, one of her confidants, the Dean of Windsor, guided the Prince on the selection of college. Dr Woods travelled to Cambridge, visited several colleges and finally recommended his own – Trinity, a royal foundation. But this was not the decisive factor: Trinity, the Queen was assured, offered the essence of Cambridge teaching. Another point in the college's favour was the fact that the Master was Lord Butler, the one-time statesman who had served the Queen. And so on Sunday, 4 December 1966, it was announced that 'the Prince of Wales has been accepted by Trinity College, Cambridge, for entry in October 1967'. The fellow appointed to direct him in his studies was Dr Denis Marrian, a Yorkshireman from Bradford and an organic chemist. Because of his own predilection for science and technology, Prince Philip perhaps secretly hoped that Charles would interest himself in some branch of science. Yet when the Prince's subjects were published at the beginning of May, it was seen that after a grounding in constitutional history and economics, his own personal choice would be pre-history (physical and social), anthropology and archaeology. From this selection it was clear that Charles was intrigued by the mode of life of early civilizations. This propensity for studying the past had expressed itself at different times, as when he explored the remains of Henry II's palace at Windsor or the Scottish cliffs in search of caveman relics while he was at Gordonstoun.

Trinity College provided the ideal setting for his interests and temperament. Not only was it rich in wealth but also in antiquity. The ebullient Henry VIII had created it, investing it with religious ideals – 'to the glory and honour of Almighty God and the Holy and Undivided Trinity for the establishment of true religion and the extirpation of heresy and the education of youth in piety, virtue, discipline and learning'. He guaranteed its prosperity and continuity with his gains from the monasteries he had sacked. Since then Trinity's association with royalty has gone unbroken.

Years ago the sovereign was received in an atmosphere of nervous tension. At mealtimes he sat remotely at High Table served by the fellow-Commoners. But it was much more a testing time for the Master, for his incumbency depended entirely on the monarch and his was the sole appointment of a master to be made by the Crown at Cambridge. The old college of King's Hall was particularly attractive to Prince Charles. Merged with Henry's foundation, it had started life in 1317 under the foundation of the first Prince of Wales. But doubtless more intimate and satisfying to him was his sense of upholding a royal tradition. As well as George VI – and his brother the Duke of Gloucester – other royal students at Trinity had been George IV, Edward VII and his son the Duke of Clarence.

Unlike his forebears, however, Charles would be the first to immerse himself wholeheartedly in Trinity's multifarious life. The others, owing to the inhibitions that royal rank had imposed upon them in those times, had resided in mansions outside the town with staffs in dutiful attendance.

That had also been the fate of Edward VII while he was at Oxford. On the occasions when he was released from his isolation he 'was obliged', the Duke of Windsor once recalled, 'in deference to the wishes of his parents, to wear the full undergraduate regalia of a "nobleman", namely, a velvet cap with gold tassels and a long, full-sleeved black gown; and when he appeared in the Oxford Union all the undergraduates would rise respectfully to their feet'.

However, the barrier between Prince and people was diminishing. Even Prince Albert Edward's appearance at Oxford was more modest than that of George IV, whose matriculation had been celebrated with a banquet. For his son's year at Oxford, the Consort had arranged to rent Frewin Hall. The Prince lived there in virtual seclusion, apart from his attendances at chapel, at times dining in hall, and entertaining meticulously chosen students to dinner. Albert Edward, unlike Prince Charles, was never the slightest bit academically inclined, and was at Oxford only long enough to be bored and 'meet the horse-copers, dog-fanciers and rat-catchers who formed the best undergraduate society'. Cunning or connivance enabled him to delight in the forbidden cigarette and, with Bishop Wilberforce, to play cards for the first time for money.

Cambridge first saw him in January 1861, living in a rented house some miles away. By now he was rebelling against the regimentation of his life and the dining companions chosen for him by others. With a sprinkling of privileged undergraduates, for a while Albert Edward visited Charles Kingsley's drawing-room for lectures on such weighty subjects as the growth of the national debt, the freedom of the press, bribery at elections and the divine right of kings. The author of *The Water Babies* no doubt spoke with characteristic animation but failed to impress his royal student. Finally, the Prince played truant.

His disappointed father remarked: 'He has a strange nature ... he has no interest in things but all the more for persons.' That was the true value of the Prince's stay at Oxford and Cambridge. They exposed him to a new world of attractive women, sport and congenial companionship, rousing dormant qualities that would be invaluable in the future in international affairs.

In like manner, it was not until he went to Oxford that the Duke of Windsor, as Prince of Wales, achieved some measure of social emancipation. He still felt it imperative, however, to reassure his father, King George v, 'as to the way I was reacting to the ... pitfalls of youth'. He informed his father: 'I never smoke more than ten cigarettes a day, generally not as many, and then only smoke in the evening after dinner with never more than two before tea ... I am also in bed by 10-30 almost every evening.'

One mentions these two former Princes of Wales to illustrate how the cocoon which had insulated royal students of the past had been shed when Prince Charles entered Trinity. Lord Butler, noted for his liberalizing influence both as Minister of Education and as Home Secretary, has since remarked: 'We were absolutely determined that Prince Charles was going to live in college and share as far as possible in the everyday life of the ordinary undergraduates.' This had been agreed upon well in advance of the day when Prince Charles and about two hundred other Trinity freshmen, each holding a card bearing his name, had been photographed so that everyone could be identified by tutors and porters. Indeed Charles himself wished to pursue a normal college life. In this democratic age, he had no illusions about himself. No one would rise when he entered

Great Hall. He would be judged on personal achievement and he had much to do to attain the scholastic eminence of some past students: Byron, Bacon and Marvell, Dryden, Thackeray and Tennyson, Newton and Rutherford, to mention only a few. Others had stalked the political arena: Balfour and Baldwin, Melbourne, Grey and Campbell-Bannerman, and the ill-fated Spencer Perceval, who had fallen to an assassin's bullet in the Palace of Westminster.

As at the other stages of his educational career, there were the expected innuendoes: the snide comments querying his academic suitability. Certain critics could not desist from implying that only his rank had won him a place at Cambridge. That may have applied to the Duke of Windsor, but it was not true of Charles. Going to Oxford straight from the Navy and the gunroom, the Duke had arrived at Magdalen College having been excused the university's entrance examination, which was known as responsions. Prince Charles, however, went to Cambridge purely on merit, having passed the requisite examinations, like the nine hundred or so students then at Trinity, the biggest of the Cambridge colleges.

It was not the Prince's qualifications that gave Trinity's authorities concern, but the fear of a nuisance: reporters, photographers and curious visitors. Years earlier the dons at Oxford had been similarly apprehensive in advance of the Duke of Windsor's arrival. For a while there had been the expected clamour, but it had eventually subsided. That was precisely the experience of Prince Charles. After his initial impact on Cambridge, public curiosity largely died out. Like other students, he moved about the city streets gowned as in hall, knowing that he would be liable to a fine of 6s 8d (as a first offender) should the proctor or his officers, the 'bulldogs', find him gownless.

Conforming to college rules, he was not permitted to buy goods on hire purchase beyond £20 without first getting permission, and in his first year he was debarred from driving a car. But Charles, like most students, was not averse to side-stepping some of the rules. Perhaps he satisfied his conscience in a roundabout way by keeping his car secretly at a house outside the city. The Master of Trinity, however, was not deceived. He has since divulged that it used to amuse him to observe the Prince of Wales walk 'ostentatiously across New Court and climb into a Land-Rover driven by his detective. I knew they were going off to pick up his car and when I told him one day that he could not fool me, his face dropped a mile.

The poor chap thought he had got away with it.'

The rooms occupied by the Prince on the second floor of New Court were not lavish, but a shade more spacious and elegant than those of most freshmen, as they had been decorated by Sandringham workmen, who had also installed a tiny kitchen. Apart from his inconspicuous bodyguard, nicknamed 'Oddjobs' (who seemed to melt into the college scene), Prince Charles had neither equerry nor valet with him. Gyps, college servants, fulfilled his menial tasks, as they did for all the other students. A bedmaker kept his small suite neat and tidy, and in advance of the Prince's arrival Lord Butler humorously disclosed to the press that aspiring women were 'panting to receive him', but bedmakers were not allowed to be beautiful.

If he had adhered strictly to custom Charles would have dined five nights each week in the Great Hall, beneath the resolute gaze of Byron and Tennyson and Henry VIII. He tried hard to fit into the throng, but the many faces that somehow seemed to focus on himself proved overwhelming. He would attempt to be amiable, engaging in conversation with those about him, but as often as not he sensed the inexorable barrier that separated him from the rest. Yet the barrier was not of his own making, for as one student admitted : 'Somehow he always behaved as though he was our social inferior and not the other way round.' Many undergraduates deliberately avoided a closer relationship, or ignored him completely, simply because they looked upon themselves as beyond the princely circle, or did not wish to be accused of playing the sycophant.

During the years since he had quit the Palace schoolroom Charles had learnt that, in certain circumstances, to be the heir apparent was to be doomed at times to moments of loneliness. This he confessed to his confidant, Lord Butler. The upshot was that he fell into the routine of having his meals sent up to his rooms, which is permissible under college rules if one can afford it. In that sense Prince Charles had no problems; his allowance was no longer restricted as it had been at Cheam and Gordonstoun. Sometimes he would cook for himself, specializing in a form of goulash, or entertain on a modest scale.

The situation must not be misconstrued, however : Prince Charles was not devoid of companionship, though in the main what became his coterie came from the public-school rather than the grammar-school sector. The intake of students from the grammar and direct-grant schools had been substantial, yet the Prince's cronies were predominantly Etonians and Wykhamists. None came from humble homes. One student, for instance, was the son of a bishop; the father of another had ambassadorial status and a third was a Queen's Counsel's son.

Together with Prince Charles, seven formed themselves into a dining club – the Wapiti Club (a wapiti being a large stag, and therefore deemed to be appropriate in view of the club's all-male character). For the dinners (for which everyone donned appropriate dress), the invitations were formal and when Charles was host he presented himself as 'Lord of the Isles'. The Prince of Wales could always resort to names without inventing them – as, for example, when the Wapitis visited a Working Men's Club to watch the Marx Brothers in the film *A Night at the Opera*. Asked at the door to give his name, the Prince wrote Charlie Chester, which was quite true, considering that he is Charles, Earl of Chester.

There is nothing to imply that these dinners were highly inebriating, as those enjoyed at Oxford by the last Prince of Wales had been. (Trying to reassure his father that his drinking habits were moderate, he had described a Bullingdon Club dinner by writing: 'Most of them got rather ... excited and I came back early. There was a good deal of champagne drunk and that accounted for it. It is interesting for me to see the various forms of amusement that undergraduates indulge in.' Maybe age stirred his conscience, for years later he wrote: 'I now recall with some shame that the real reason for my early departure ... was the fact that I was no longer so steady on my feet or so clear in my speech as I was when we sat down to dinner. I hasten to add that this was an unusual occurrence, prompted only by the unwritten law of the Bullingdon Club that the new members should be forced to drink themselves into oblivion.')

Charles did get involved in a few harmless japes, among them a midnight bicycle race round the college's seventeenth-century courtyard after dining with his student friends. Yet even with the aid of mellow wine and convivial company, he could not cast off his deep-seated reserve entirely. At times, therefore, his contribution was noticeably restricted or even non-existent, especially when talk dwelt on more personal matters concerning family life. One member of this exclusive clique has described Charles as easy-going and superficially not difficult to understand. Yet deep down he was by nature a very private person, allowing no one other than the very closest intimates to crack that protective shell – 'Not that he is stand-offish in any way, and he certainly never pulled rank on any-one.'

In fact this was yet another illustration of the Prince's long struggle against inherited introspection. Although in recent years he had gained in self-confidence, he would confess towards the end of his period at Cambridge that he was 'still fairly shy'. He is more at ease with older people, yet also adores the other end of the age spectrum – young children.

If anything it was some of the local citizens – despite good inten-tions – who threatened to upset the Prince's unruffled routine. But Lord Butler tactfully and firmly countered any attempt to lionize him. The college itself accepted the princely presence with almost cloistral calm, largely, as one of Charles's contemporaries had said, because 'Trinity is intellectually a very arrogant place and not the sort of college which is going to get madly excited by the mere fact that the Prince of Wales was in residence'. That was fortunate for Prince Charles, for in that climate of scholastic haughtiness he escaped all serious pressures. His conscientious application to his studies, coupled with an irrepressible sense of humour, was his strongest asset in maintaining personal buoyancy and stability.

And always, if necessary, there was the Master of Trinity to con-sult. A potential monarch must be led carefully through the com-plexities of the political and constitutional maze. Sir Henry Marten of Eton and King George VI himself had eased these taxing labours for the Queen. Now the Prince of Wales turned to Lord Butler for similar direction. Lord Butler was an admirable mentor, having ex-perienced thirty-five years in politics, often in high office, and twice coming near to grasping the supreme prize of the premiership. Often in the evenings the Prince would visit the Master in his study, dis-cussing politics, and listening to lucid expositions of the varied aspects of the constitution and what would be required of him when he wore the crown. Both in temperament and in mental outlook there was an excellent *rapport* between the future king and the one-time minister, whose decades of public service were filled with social and educational reform.

Learning to know what a sovereign can or cannot do is a gradual process and, as Prince Charles explains in his humorous style, one learns 'the way the monkey learns: watching its parents. On the whole you pick it up as you go along.' In the same way as the

Queen served her apprenticeship from childhood with her father, King George VI, so too has Prince Charles been slowly introduced to the requirements of kingship. He added to his knowledge of constitutional history while at Gordonstoun, but reading books is a tedious and unsatisfactory way of grappling with such a complicated and sophisticated subject, certainly for the young. It is only by discussion with people who have been totally immersed in the technicalities of the constitution that the necessary knowledge is acquired.

In most matters Prince Charles veers towards the traditional and conservative point of view, but in 1968 much occurred on university campuses that tried to disrupt the standards that he symbolizes. Many colleges, both in Britain and abroad, suffered the shock of extreme socialism, and even Trinity was not immune. The Establishment, in which the Prince of Wales is necessarily a dominant figure, was under attack; the long-haired student Left frenetically shouted for change, omitting to offer a substitute for the system they wished to destroy.

Rightly or wrongly, politics are a salient facet of college activity and if Prince Charles was to identify himself completely with Trinity life, it was natural that he should participate. Indeed as a student Stanley Baldwin, the future prime minister, had been expelled from Trinity's debating society for failing to speak in debates. Members of the royal family, however, must by the nature of their impartial role hold themselves aloof from the political cockpit. Charles found himself in a quandary. When he consulted Lord Butler on the course he should take, the Master of Trinity confirmed that the heir apparent could not publicly ally himself to any political group. He advised him, however, not to dissociate himself completely, but 'to look in on college politics: that will show you basic political processes at work'.

On Lord Butler's advice, it is said, the Prince introduced himself to the President of the Trinity Student Union, Hywel Jones, the son of a Non-conformist minister whose left-wing ideals were vehemently expressed in Welsh oratory. Prince Charles and Jones represented worlds that were poles apart. This, plus the intolerance of youth, might have led immediately to mutual dislike. Yet contrary to expectations, a firm friendship grew. Occupying nearby rooms, they often discussed political issues far into the night. Such talks left a profound impression on the Prince of Wales, who was now inclined to modify his conservatism. With others who could speak from eye-witness experience, Jones was later to resent the insinuation that Charles graduated more by a fluke rather than by personal industry.

In moments of relaxation Charles still cherished his schoolboy pastime of music. He also began to pilot an aircraft. And being so near, he could also shoot on the Sandringham estate, as a farmhouse at Wolferton had been modernized for his weekend use. He tried to merge inconspicuously into college activity, and in writing an article for the student newspaper he appreciated with typical good sense that it 'received an unfair proportion of publicity for its literary and descriptive quality'. When therefore he was offered an annual payment of £10,000 to write articles for a national newspaper, he knew that it was not in tribute to his literary powers but solely a means of capitalizing on his rank.

His love of the theatre inevitably drew him to the college stage. Before leaving Gordonstoun he had played the part of the Pirate King in *The Pirates of Penzance*. Now, at Trinity, there was the chance to exploit his passion for Goon humour – in the college revue *Revulution* which, according to the Prince, was full of 'groan jokes'. But, he asked himself, could he, the heir apparent, really take part in a frivolous cabaret? Again he consulted Trinity's Master, who advised him to participate. Inevitably the time was approaching when he would be compelled to make public speeches; it was essential, therefore, that he should 'learn how to deliver throw-away lines'. Lord Butler has since declared that the lessons learnt in *Revulution* contributed handsomely to the Prince's achievements in public. In turn, the Prince is adamant that he learnt the actor's sense of timing – an essential rudiment of public speaking – on Trinity's stage.

The Prince appeared in fourteen of forty items in the revue. In the most publicized sketch, he sat in a dustbin and was interviewed about a prominent college freshman called 'Reg Sprott' – the name given by Charles to a dustman who sang under his rooms in the early morning. In one lampoon he strode on stage shouting, 'I wreak vengeance', while another player ran past, holding his nose, and remarking: 'So that's what it is.' Charles raised an umbrella and confided to the audience: 'I lead a sheltered life', and, grinning lewdly, arm in arm with a girl, he whispered: 'I like to give myself heirs.'

Work, however, outmatched diversions. Whereas many students attended no more than half the lectures, the Prince was rarely absent. At one point, before going to Cambridge, the thought of reading for the Tripos was alien to him, yet, confounding the cynics, he finally graduated with a BA (Hons.) degree in history. Lord Butler has declared that the Prince's scholastic achievement would have been greater but for the interruption of royal functions in his final year. The Master of Trinity had hoped that Charles would pursue his studies without intervention. For that reason he did not quite approve when the Queen and Prince Philip decided that, while still reading history, Charles should spend one term at the University College of Wales. He was to be invested as Prince of Wales and, unlike his immediate predecessors, he was to acquire a knowledge of the Welsh language and culture.

Many citizens of Wales waxed jubilant at the thought that their Prince was to reside among them; but not all shared their delight. To the Free Wales Army, anxious to rid itself of the English yoke, Prince Charles — Carlo Windsor, as they christened him — symbolized centuries of English imperialism. In the secrecy of their mountain hide-outs they began to fashion their bombs.

5 Culture and Ceremonial

Aberystwyth is an attractive watering-place standing at the western end of the Vale of Rheidol, near the confluences of the rivers Ystwith and Rheidol, and in roughly the centre of Cardigan Bay. Set on the rugged western coast of Wales, it has for centuries contributed to Welsh history. On a promontory to the south-west of the town lie the ruins of its ancient castle, erected in 1277 by the astute and war-like Edward I, who gave Welshmen their first English Prince of Wales. They rise from the site of a fortress of great strength, built by one Gilbert de Strongbow, and destroyed by Owen Gwynedd, a name revered by Welshmen.

That was centuries ago. Today the dominant influence on Aberystwyth is the University College of Wales gazing out over the bay, whose students account for a quarter of its population. Numbering some 2,300, they live about a mile inland, in the grey stone Pant-y-Celyn hall of residence, set among attractively laid-out grounds. Here, complying with a whim of the Welsh Office in London's Whitehall, Prince Charles would live for three months, appeasing Welsh nationalism by studying its language. It was to be the prelude to his investiture as Prince of Wales.

As at all times in his education, preferential treatment was denied to him on instructions from Buckingham Palace. Even a warden's double room that had been set aside was instead allocated to his personal detective. Charles himself was assigned to a room of more modest dimensions.

Conscientious as ever, with the assistance of Mr Cledwyn Hughes, then Secretary of State for Wales, he had begun to absorb himself in the history and culture of the Welsh – even delving a little into the mysteries of their language – before going to Cambridge. Therefore on his arrival in Aberystwyth on 20 April 1969 he had some vague inkling of the snags that lay in store. What were as yet unknown to him were the future antics, if any, of the Free

Wales Army. No one knew whether to take their threats and fanaticism seriously or not. Perhaps their much-publicized intentions to assassinate were merely puerile outpourings prompted by frustrated nationalist aims. But always there was an atmosphere of tension and the authorities could not be sure. It was seen in the demonstrations and the waving placards, the release of a record of an offensive song, and the hunger strike of four students who backed the nationalist cause.

Faced with the risk of personal injury, perhaps Charles wondered why he should be a pawn in the political game. Apart from that, how anyone could become fluent in a highly complex language in three months was beyond normal comprehension. But sanity is sometimes absent from the politician's mind when there is the chance of political gain. Mr Gwynfor Evans, president of the Welsh Nationalist Party, had shocked the Labour Party by triumphing over its candidate in a by-election at Carmarthen. And now Prince Charles was to be exploited in an attempt to stem the socialist rot.

Political chicanery angered Mr A. J. P. Taylor, the historian, who thundered in a newspaper article that the 'prestige of the Monarchy and its secure position above the parties are injured by this sordid exploitation of the Monarchy for party reasons'. Mr Evans, though less impassioned, admitted that the pending investiture did not excite him, stressing that the title Prince of Wales

'... had been a powerful and emotive title in Welsh history and, following the two hundred years' struggle of the Welsh against the Norman-English order, it was taken by Edward I and given to his eldest son in order to weaken Welsh resistance and to pave the way for integrating the Welsh nation in the English state. Not unnaturally I am unenthusiastic about this. The situation would be quite different if Wales had Commonwealth status, in which case the Queen of England would be Queen of Wales, as she is the Queen of Canada, Australia and New Zealand when she goes to those countries.'

One could not dismiss the nationalist threat of terrorism. Already in recent years there had been ten explosions; indeed the last bomb had exploded at the police headquarters in Cardiff a mere five days before Charles's arrival in Wales. Sensibly the Queen had a team of Special Branch officers assigned as protection. Billeted in the town and posing as students, they mingled with the people unobtrusively, eavesdropping in public places. Implementing them was a bomb-disposal expert from Chester, and Commander Albert Perkins, the

Queen's own detective, twice visited Abersytwyth to reassure himself that security was as sound as it could be.

Charles stoically accepted the situation, quite aware that if an attempt was to be made on his life there was ample opportunity. At times, for instance, hundreds of people lined the route when he drove to the college itself, a habit that a warden once likened to the morbid curiosity once seen at public hangings.

The Prince's stoutest armour was his simple, captivating charm and the sincerity with which he managed to identify himself with the Welsh. When he spoke in Welsh at the National Eisteddfod of the Urdd in Aberystwyth, for most of the people his popularity was complete; they christened him '*cariad bach*' – 'little darling'.

Dr Thomas Parry, then the Principal, has since explained that the College gave a number of dinners for local people to meet the Prince. What was conspicuous was the way he was 'completely relaxed and pleasant. He has his father's flair for interesting conversation. Everyone was very impressed not only with his naturalness and lack of formality but with his interest in things around him and his good sense. The Prince was very much the student, keeping up his Cambridge studies by writing weekly essays ... He has thought deeply about some of the great problems of our time and is genuinely concerned about solving them.'

There was considerable scope for the Prince's interest in Welsh affairs in the many organizations hankering after royal patronage. He readily championed the 'Countryside in 1970' campaign, presiding over the Prince of Wales Committee, which is concerned with protecting the environment in Wales. His passion for all things rural caused him to speak with ardour, emphasizing that his object was

'... to be alarmist and to say that there is a very small line between extinction and survival – and this applies to the country as well – and that legislation should be enacted now and not vaguely in the future. In South Wales nearly an acre disappears under mine wastage every three days. I could go on until I am blue in the face and you are, I hope, aware of many of the problems. An enormous percentage of the population of Britain and of Wales seems to be totally unaware except when it is too late. The most distressing aspect about the whole question is the dormant state of public opinion in this country. If it could be awakened somehow, the whole task of making our environment habitable would be immeasurably easier.'

These words convey the emotionalism of the self-confessed romantic.

The purpose of the Prince's stay in Wales had been greeted with scepticism. For Charles it was a delicate testing time, with both personal achievement and disaster in the balance. Apparently even his curriculum was rather nebulous when he first arrived. Mr Arfon Owen, the registrar, has revealed that there was 'a certain coyness about the object of the exercise, and it was never made clear. If he had been thoroughly stupid it would have been awful. But he kept up with his British history, studied Welsh history and literature, as well as the language. No one but a gifted mimic could have learnt to pronounce it so well. In effect, his time in Wales was an extended Royal Tour, but there's no class-consciousness here which makes it rather difficult for the monarchy.'

This last sentence does not tally with events. Prince Charles had gone to Wales with some trepidation, adding:

'If one takes this as it comes it will be much easier. I expect at Aberystwyth there may be one or two demonstrations, and as long as I don't get covered too much in egg and tomato I'll be all right, but I don't blame people demonstrating like that. They have never seen me before, they do not know what I am like. I have hardly been to Wales, and you really can't expect people to be over zealous about the fact of having a so-called English Prince to come amongst them and be frightfully excited. Once I have been there for eight weeks things might improve.'

As predicted, there were demonstrations, but nothing worse. As for lack of class-consciousness, by the time the Prince of Wales wrote out a cheque for £85 – £20 for tuition and £65 for accommodation – on 22 June, the University College of Wales had exhausted its prospectuses. The three months' residence of a royal student had made this Welsh foundation fashionable; there were as many as 10,000 applicants for the 670 available places, more than 2,000 up on the previous year.

Charles had completed with distinction the first phase of his Welsh Odyssey. The second phase – the investiture – would be a much more prickly affair. Some people would scoff at it as political ballyhoo, but Prince Charles regarded it 'as being a meaningful ceremony'. Cynics and politicians apart, for himself it would be a launching-pad into public life. Anticipation was not without strain. The Prince of Wales confessed that he would be glad when the ceremony was over, because 'having spent a year in the midst of controversy and talk, between one side and another, it has become a friction point for many people'.

Catarrhal sinusitis had prevented the Queen from opening the British Empire and Commonwealth Games in Cardiff on 26 July 1958. Prince Philip, however, had introduced Her Majesty's recorded message, which, prepared by the British Broadcasting Corporation, ran: 'I want to take this opportunity of speaking to all Welsh people, not only in this arena, but wherever they may be. The British Empire and Commonwealth Games in the capital, together with all the activities of the Festival of Wales, have made a memorable year for the principality. I have, therefore, to mark it further by an act which will, I hope, give as much pleasure to all Welshmen as it does to me. I intend to create my son, Charles, Prince of Wales today. When he is grown up I will present him to you at Caernarvon.'

Only a smattering of people, among them Commonwealth prime ministers and Charles himself, knew in advance of the statement that Prince Charles, then nine years and eight months old, heard on the radio in his headmaster's study at Cheam. He had accepted with characteristic equanimity the prospect of being the focal point of an ancient distinction, but how he contemplated the investiture then is not known. It had certainly disconcerted the last title-holder, his great-uncle, the Duke of Windsor. 'This ceremony', the Duke revealed in his memoirs, 'had been allowed to lapse for centuries, but surprisingly enough the Welsh radical, Mr David Lloyd George, who only a few years before shocked my family with his famous Limehouse speech attacking inherited privilege, decided that its revival would appeal to the national pride of his people. With an eye to what would please his constituents, Lloyd George proposed that the ceremony be transformed into a spectacular Welsh pageant.' The idea of wearing period dress appalled him. He wrote:

'The ceremony I had to go through, with the speech I had to make, and the Welsh I had to speak were, I thought, a sufficient ordeal for anyone. But when a tailor appeared to measure me for a fantastic costume designed for the occasion, consisting of white satin breeches and mantle and surcoat of purple velvet edged with ermine, I decided things had gone too far.

'I had already submitted to the Garter dress and robe, for which there existed a condoning historical precedent; but what would my Navy friends say if they saw me in this preposterous rig?

'There was a family blow-up that night; but in the end my mother, as always, smoothed things over. I also got the impression, although the thought was never actually put into words, that if I did what was asked of me it would help Papa in his dealings with the difficult Mr Lloyd George.'

In fairness to everyone concerned, the Duke, then seventeen, and devoid of the instinctive taste for dressing up of his grandfather, King Edward VII, was opposed to all ceremonial. In his diary, for instance, he recorded that state visits were unreal shows of ceremony, rot and a waste of time and energy.

Today those items of period dress that roused such acute princely resentment in 1911 are exhibited in the National Museum of Wales. While in Cardiff Prince Philip inspected them closely in silence, and is said to have carried on without comment. Maybe he recalled the childhood scene when Prince Charles energetically refused to appear in a page's dress at a royal wedding. Prince Charles would, however, adopt a more moderate approach to his role than his predecessor. Yet as his investiture approached, he betrayed a hint of trepidation. In a radio interview he remarked: 'It would be unnatural, I think, if one did not feel any apprehension about it. One always wonders what is going to happen in this sort of thing. But I think if one takes this as it comes, it will be much easier.'

He omitted to mention his Welsh ancestry. Maybe at that time he was unaware of it – certainly in detail. The excitement of the pre-investiture period, however, gave the stimulus for people to probe his lineage in dusty archives. Major Francis Jones, Wales Herald Extraordinary and county archivist at Carmarthen, now revealed that Richard II – a former Princes of Wales and son of the Black Prince – was directly descended from the Welsh warrior princes, and that Charles's ancestry could be traced to the fifteenth-century Owen Glendower, Wales's most romantic hero. The link with Owen is traceable through two daughters and two sisters, down to the fifth Earl of Cumberland, the third Earl of Cork, and, indeed, the Queen Mother. Other ancestral threads emanated from Gruffydd-ap-Cynam, Llewellyn, Bleddyn-ap-Cynfyn and Hywel Dda, who codified the Welsh laws.

Capitalizing on this romantic past Caernarvon, which looks out towards the island of Anglesey from the foot of the Menai Strait, had assumed over the centuries the honour of honorary Welsh capital; or so it seemed. Agricola had founded it in AD 78 as the fort of Segontium, marking the north-west extremity of the Roman Empire. Then after subjugating the Welsh princes the doughty warrior Edward I built the magnificent castle with money borrowed from Lombardy bankers. Altogether it cost about £19,000 – in excess of £2 million at today's values and reflecting its strategic value as a military fortification and offices to administer and control Wales. For more than a century there dwelt in this massive walled garrison, with its huge eagle dominating the main tower to mirror former Roman might, sixty-four English burgesses.

Given such long-standing eminence as the vice-regal hub of conquest, one could readily appreciate why the people of Caernarvon claimed that their town was the capital of Wales. Yet soon after the Second World War the borough, with typical Welsh fervour, petitioned King George VI in the following words:

'... Welsh is the language of the town. In its corporate and individual life it radiates all that is truest, finest and noblest in the nation ... Religion, art, drama, and music find in it a worthy home. Caernarvon, more than any other town or city in the Principality, can claim to represent truly the Welsh way of life ...

'Wales, like every other nation and civilised country in the world, needs a capital town. The absence of such has been a retarding factor in the life of the nation.

'Your petitioners humbly, but proudly, recall that the first Prince of Wales was born in Caernarvon, and that in 1911 King George V graciously acceded to hold the Investiture of the Prince of Wales in their town.

'Your petitioners maintain that Caernarvon is the recognized and traditional capital of Wales, and that the Welsh nation would be pleased and gratified if Your Majesty recognized the right of the Principality to its own capital, and by reason of the prerogative vested in Your Majesty, grant the privilege of Letters Patent under the Great Seal to the Borough of Caernarvon.'

But there were other petitions for this distinction, from Cardiff, Aberystwyth and Llandrindod Wells. In the end it was Cardiff who received capital status. Aberystwyth was acknowledged as the seat of learning and Caernarvon's claim to be the nation's ceremonial focal-point was established. On 9 August 1963 Queen Elizabeth II bestowed on Caernarvon a further honour. From the borough's historic limestone pile she announced: 'Felly penodaf Caernarfon i fod yn Fwrdeisdref Frenhinol', which means in English, 'I therefore declare Caernarvon to be a royal borough.'

Thus after a lapse of many years the stage was set, with the requisite properties and scenic décor, for the Welsh to receive their prince. The date of the investiture was to be 1 July 1969. But when the Queen promised to present her son to the people of Wales at Caernarvon, she neither assured nor contemplated what would irreverently be described as a 'national extravaganza'. Until the time of the Stuarts, the Prince of Wales had been invested either in Parliament or in one of the English towns. Maybe through apathy, or through crass ignorance of English ways – and certainly in no small measure to their animosity towards their first born – the Hanoverian monarchs had virtually confined the investiture to the issuing of letters patent.

Yet change was on its way. In 1889 Alfred Edwards, Bishop of Asaph, who was eventually raised to the archbishopric of Wales, talked over tea at Windsor Castle of the desirability of a ceremony focusing on the unity of England and Wales. Either Queen Victoria or her politicians were unreceptive, but in due course the bishop's notion found fertility elsewhere. When King George V succeeded to the throne in 1910 that wily Welshman David Lloyd George, then Chancellor of the Exchequer, saw in a lavish spectacle the vehicle for self-aggrandizement in the eyes of the constituents, and seized on Edwards' proposal for the investiture of the next Prince of Wales. As he was the member for Caernarvon and Constable of the castle, it does seem that Lloyd George was influenced by political motives. Perhaps, too, it was a ploy by this articulate reformer to appease many who had been offended by his waspish attacks on ancient traditions.

Thus in July 1911 the seventeen-year-old midshipman-prince, who had passed through the naval school at Osborne (where he was nicknamed 'Sardine') and had entered Dartmouth as a naval cadet, interrupted his studies and on a

'... sweltering day within the vast ruin of Caernarvon Castle, before some ten thousand people, with Winston Churchill as Home Secretary mellifluously proclaiming my titles (he told me afterwards that he rehearsed them on the golf course), my father invested me as Prince of Wales. Upon my head he put a coronet cap as token of principality, and in to my hand the gold verge of government, and on my middle finger the gold ring of responsibility. Then leading me by the hand through an archway to one of the towers of the battlements, he presented me to the people of Wales. Half fainting with heat and nervousness, I delivered the Welsh sentences that Mr. Lloyd George, standing close by in the ancient garb of Constable, had taught me.'

The shy and sensitive Prince Edward had viewed the pomp with chagrin and embarrassment. If Prince Charles secretly hoped to avoid a similar Welsh 'spectacular' he was disappointed; by all accounts the Welsh Office and 'Uncle George' (Mr George Thomas, then Secretary of State for Wales) insisted on a show. Subsequent cynicism was therefore unfortunate – and misleading. In his book *The Prince, the Crown and the Cash*, Mr Emrys Hughes wrongly claimed: 'Although the Secretary for Wales took the view that the main purpose of the investiture was to boost the Welsh tourist industry, there was another view that it would give a boost to the Prince, and Royalty, preparatory to a campaign for an increase in the Civil List (the allowance made annually to the Crown).' Nothing could have been more alien to fact. In the Queen's view the 1911 investiture was much too ostentatious even for those times, and utterly out of character with the simpler royal mode of today. Moreover there was the inevitable question of cost: the Queen queried the need to expend so large a sum of money and, to effect economies, suggested that the procession should be dispensed with. 'She would have said no to the whole thing, if she could,' someone connected with the planning is alleged to have said.

At first it was estimated that the investiture would cost in the neighbourhood of £500,000 but the figure later shrank to £200,000. (After the ceremony the government gave a final figure of £130,000.) But the hereditary Earl Marshal, the Duke of Norfolk, the major domo in such matters, wrote to the Prime Minister: 'It was meant to be a help, not a hindrance. I said that from what I'd heard it might come to more than £200,000 and we may have to have, what's the phrase, a supplementary estimate.'

In the initial stages at least, the investiture roused little or no enthusiasm among many of the Welsh. If one accepts the accuracy of a survey conducted in September 1968 by the National Research Centre for the *Western Mail*, forty-four per cent of the people interviewed thought that the forthcoming investiture and the accompanying celebrations were a mere squandering of public money. A third, furthermore, also accused the monarchy of not changing with the times. This charge was, of course, totally untrue; indeed the salient reason for the British monarchy's survival (whereas most European dynasties have collapsed) is because down the centuries it has changed – sometimes, one must admit, under coercion – according to the wishes of the nation. In common parlance, it moved with the times to keep in step with the majority voice of public opinion. It was for that reason that the resistance of the Queen and Prince Philip against costly pageantry melted away.

'I think,' explained Prince Philip during an interview on Grampian Television, 'the doubts are not so much allowing him [Prince

Charles] to take part at all, but if we had any doubts, perhaps to what extent this sort of virtually medieval revival was relevant, and I think that probably the final governing factor was that it was quite obvious that a very large proportion of Welsh opinion favoured this. This really tipped the scales.' Events would prove convincingly the reality of Prince Philip's words. Cynicism seemed to evaporate before a torrent of public ecstasy. 'The support of the populace exceeded my wildest dreams,' rhapsodized the Secretary of State for Wales. 'I don't want to be guilty of the Welsh sin of exaggeration, but it was a far greater triumph than we had a right to expect. He really was the Prince Charming. Wales has been in a state of euphoria, and at least half a million dollars came to Caernarvon itself.'

But long before the momentous day the investiture had to be planned. And so in September 1967 an Investiture Office appeared in London, and the Duke of Norfolk presided over the deliberations of a huge committee. 'There will be no monkeying about in the name of modernization,' warned the traditionalist Earl Marshal, who, to solve some of his problems, used toy soldiers and also organized rehearsals in the grounds of Buckingham Palace. And when the investiture was over, he could say : 'I did not change one iota of the ceremony from 1911 because that would have been wrong. It is a constitutional act, and as such you cannot do it. I frankly believe it could not have gone better. There is still a great sense of pride in this country, thank God.'

The Earl of Snowdon was chosen to stage-manage the ceremony in the castle grounds, and made simplicity the overruling motif – 'to let the castle speak for itself, and have the dais as a kind of theatre in the round so that it would read well on colour television'. One concession to modernity was a canopy of acrylic sheets that, spread over the dais, was held up by steel rods in the style of lances – a design guaranteed to withstand fierce gales. Indeed in a wind tunnel a scale model had endured the strain of sixty-mile-an-hour gusts. More important, for the first time in the ceremony's centuries-old history there was the intrusion of the television camera, making the investiture a world event, seen by over five hundred million viewers. Fifty tons of turf were even laid to enhance the colourful robes when they were transmitted on the television screen.

A desire for simplicity, plus the uncompromising limitations imposed by television, restricted the guests to about four thousand, less than half the number in 1911. Of these three thousand five hundred formed a detailed cross-section of Welsh life. Unhappily lack of co-ordination between the television companies added substantially to costs and led to a surfeit of cameras. For a six-hour programme the British Broadcasting Corporation used more than thirty cameras and allied equipment valued at about £2 million. The resources of commercial television were much more modest. In *The Times* the chairman of Independent Television's special events enlightened: 'More than fifty cameras were doing the work of twenty-five. Attempts to bring reason to bear upon this absurd situation failed.'

Although the Queen had questioned the need for an occasion of splendour, with its commensurate cost, the politicians distributed public largesse with generous zeal. Yet it could be argued that the outlay was justified, if we assess it against the subsequent gain from tourism and in other ways. In any event the government allocated £115,000 for all requirements at Caernarvon Castle; to the Ministry of Defence went £40,000 to cope with the cost of 2,500 troops (including 148 men and 170 horses of the Household Cavalry, and to constructing a temporary bridge across the river at Caernarvon). Car parks and mobile public lavatories involved expenditure of £36,000, and the cost of conveying Commonwealth representatives and ambassadors to Caernarvon by train totalled £4,000. A similar sum was allocated as expenses to the Earl Marshal's office, and £2,000 went in preparing Griffiths Crossing, some two and a half miles from Caernarvon, where the royal party would proceed to the castle. Again the Queen had asked if this was really necessary, offering to go straight to Caernarvon railway station and to omit the procession; there would then have been no need to use the Windsor greys. But the Welsh Office was not to be dissuaded from staging its regal display and attendant sumptuousness.

In London the College of Arms, delving into the records of investitures of other ages, pored over the account of the 1610 ceremony of Henry, heir to James I, and noted that more or less the same ritual was repeated six years later for Henry's brother, the future Charles I. Sir Anthony Wagner, Garter King of Arms, is on record as saying: 'Until 1621 peers were always invested, but James I and Buckingham (desperately attempting to raise money to by-pass Parliament) were selling off so many (a barony cost £15,000) that they had to do away with the ceremony. The investiture of the Prince of Wales is a special form of investiture for a peer. It could be done anywhere. Doing it in Wales is purely a political gesture.' This political zeal infected others. The Mayor of Caernarvon, having cast off his earlier scepticism, said:

'You could put a suit of armour on that boy, and send him to Agincourt. I reckon he's the ace in the royalist pack. Wales has reached a point where we need friends – from Buckingham Palace upwards, or downwards. The investiture is the spur that has got us to do things we wouldn't ordinarily have done. We've put a shilling on the rates and begun a crash programme for the streets. It's a bit like asking a village to run a cup final, but life would be very dull if we didn't have any pageantry. The castle, of course, is not a symbol of oppression, but of our toughness ... There's no oppressor any more. It's a privilege for the Prince, as well as the Principality.'

The borough council voted £3,000 for decorations, a local firm gave 5,000 pounds of paint to the townsfolk and ancient Caernarvon was adorned afresh.

As at coronations, the investiture was seen by some as a means of capitalizing on history. Officialdom gave its blessing to the sale of 166 items: pie funnels and cruet sets, tiles, goblets and tankards, pendants, pill-boxes and paperweights, napkin rings, tree plaques and crystal chalices, rugs and dolls and so on. The more affluent could buy a silver cigar container for £100; a commemorative vase realized £5 more. In terraced houses landladies charged £5 per person (two in a room) and hotel bookings reached capacity well in advance. One person even sold pieces of Snowdonia at £4 a square foot, together with an illuminated scroll.

Not all, however, were caught up in the swift current of civic exuberance. The forty thousand members of Plaid Cymru, the national party, pledged themselves to ostracize the Prince and gelignite was offered for sale at £3 for a two-ounce stick. Not a few were apprehensive about his safety. Apart from the threat of assassination, rebellious gestures were rather puerile, with the Prince, for instance, being caricatured as an obedient dog and dubbed 'this German oaf' in pamphlets of the Free Wales Army. For those who wished to vent their spleen in satire, there was the song:

> I have a friend who lives in Buckingham Palace
> And Carlo Windsor is his name
> The last time I went round to his house
> His mother answered the door and said:
> 'Carlo, Carlo, Carlo is playing polo today

Carlo is playing polo with his Daddy.'
So come all ye serfs of Wales and join in the chorus
At last you have a prince in the land of song.

While the dissidents confined their activities to painting, here and there, the words 'Revolution in Progress', or blotting out road signs in English, there was no need to be alarmed. But on 17 November 1967 a bomb exploded at Cardiff's Temple of Peace, where 450 Welshmen had gathered to discuss the investiture. It would be the first of thirteen incidents involving bombs, the last occurring some hours before the Prince was invested.

Altogether a sum of about £23,000 was disbursed on security. Hours before the ceremony numerous policemen mingled inconspicuously with the crowds. To enter the space beneath the seats in the castle, whose arrow-slits were boarded over, one had to pass through doors equipped with M15 security locks. In the streets manhole covers were made immovable. The false rumour that the Prince of Wales was to don a bullet-proof vest irritated him enormously. Even so, the security authorities could not guarantee him against incidents. Only the previous day a homemade bomb – a wrist watch and two sticks of gelignite – had exploded at Cardiff Post Office, though fortunately no one had come to harm. And on the day when Charles received his princely crown, two terrorists – a painter and a roadworker – were their own victims at Abergele and not the local government offices they had proposed to destroy in protest at the Caernarvon ceremony.

Nothing could be left to chance – not even a parcel lurking behind a tent in an army camp on the processional route; some fifty soldiers were evacuated at once but the contents were a harmless yellow sou'wester. Similarly the Queen and her family, travelling overnight in the purple-painted royal train, were delayed for an hour at Crewe: a time-bomb had been located under a bridge near Chester, but specialists found it to be a stupid hoax – two sticks of Plasticine attached to a clock. When the royal coaches finally came to a halt they stood in a siding near Bangor. On one side were cliffs and the Menai Strait; on the other, a wooded valley. Throughout the night security men had searched the track as far as Griffiths Crossing.

At 10.45 on the morning of 1 July, the royal family disembarked for a champagne breakfast with Sir Michael Duff, Lord Lieutenant of Caernarvonshire, at Vaynol, his mansion overlooking the Menai

Strait. Here armed police patrolled the grounds. Sir Michael has recalled:

'[The] Queen looked dreadfully tense but not Prince Charles; if he had any nerves, he hid them extremely well. In fact, at one point the Queen asked me, "Where on earth has Charles got to?" and I said, "Well, Ma'am, I think he's gone off to look at a horse of mine he's interested in"; he took the whole thing extraordinarily calmly. Indeed, at one stage Prince Charles was wandering in from the garden, caught sight of himself on television and remarked cheerfully: "It's always me – I'm getting rather bored with my face".'

That day only official vehicles entered Caernarvon after 3 am, and along the Menai Strait police officers in rubber dinghies searched for a possible bomb. A couple of minesweepers were also active not far out, and as the thousands of onlookers began their patient wait, a television camera relentlessly scrutinized them from the roof of a police van, while observers in three helicopters kept watch from five hundred feet.

As a preview the teeming crowds had watched the television interview with Prince Charles, but now they saw him in person. The procession began outside the premises of the County Council where, on the roof, a detective, equipped with binoculars and short-wave radio, observed the spectators. In the Prince's carriage, escorted by Household Cavalry, were his equerry and the Secretary of State for Wales. On their way to the castle a bomb exploded, startling the occupants in the following cars, but injuring none, and over the Eagle Tower the Prince's personal banner – bearing the arms of the last native prince – was broken as State Trumpeters of the Household Cavalry in groups of eight sounded a fanfare from the battlements. As he walked to the Chamberlain Tower to await the summons from the Queen, the audience broke lustily into *God Bless the Prince of Wales*:

> Among our ancient mountains
> And from our lovely vales,
> Oh, let the prayer re-echo,
> God bless the Prince of Wales.

Meanwhile, as the Queen's coach rumbled along the route, a youth threw a banana skin beneath the horses' hooves, an act of folly that accentuated jangled nerves. To rescue him from furious sightseers, the police hauled him away to the courthouse, where he was fined £3 for insulting behaviour. There would be no more bombs – only the sound of gunfire in salute, mingling with the clattering hooves of the Household Cavalry.

Knocking on the Water Gate, Lord Plunkett sought admission in the name of the Queen. The response was theatrical rather than ceremonial. As the door opened the Earl of Snowdon was seen holding an oak-tray bearing an enormous key (fifteen inches long and six and a half pounds in weight] – an innovation introduced by Lloyd George at the last investiture to impress. Said Lord Snowdon: 'Madam, I surrender the key of this castle into your Majesty's hand.' Touching the key, the Queen replied: 'Sir Constable, I return the key of this castle into your keeping.' The royal banner having replaced that of Prince Charles, the Queen's procession – brilliant, despite grey skies, with the trappings of ancient garb – slowly made its way to the dais. There were the great officers of state, the Heralds, Service chiefs and, of course, the Home Secretary, the Rt Hon James Callaghan.

Patriotism having expressed itself volubly in the Welsh and English anthems, the Earl Marshal, at the Queen's request, directed Garter King of Arms to summon Prince Charles. Happily the Prince had been spared the sartorial fussiness of the long cumbersome train and satin breeches that had so annoyed the Duke of Windsor. Instead his dress was more in the spirit of the Welsh: the ceremonial uniform of the Royal Regiment of Wales, of which he is colonel-in-chief. The collar badges symbolized the South Wales Borderers and the Welch Regiment (which comprised the new regiment), the red dragon of Wales and the wreath of immortelles of the Borderers – a memento of victory over the French.

The procession from the Chamberlain Tower itself upheld the pageantry. With the Prince were the Wales Herald Extraordinary, the Secretary of State for Wales and two supporting peers for the Prince. Five Welsh peers bore the insignia. Earl Lloyd George of Dwyfor carried the silver-gilt sword used at the last investiture and inscribed with the name of the previous title-holder. In the possession of Lord Heycock was the two-foot-eight-inch golden rod, or verge, in silver gilt, decorated with cupids and ostrich feathers. The golden ring, displaying two lively dragons clutching an amethyst, was in the safe keeping of Lord Maelor. Lord Harlech bore the mantle of purple silk velvet trimmed with ermine and sealskin dots and, most important of all, Lord Ogmore carried the coronet.

These five emblems bridged the years to the day when Henry of

Monmouth, later Henry V, victor of Agincourt, had himself been invested. But they were not the same insignia, most of the royal jewels having suffered the common fate of being sold or melted down during the Commonwealth. As in other days, the sword signified defence; the rod, authority; and the ring symbolized that the Prince of Wales, wedded to his country, was the father of her children. The gold clasp worn by the previous Prince of Wales enriched the mantle.

But what arrested attention most of all was the coronet, not only by its starkness but because it was the product of modern science. Donated by the Goldsmiths' Company and designed to the specification of the Prince's namesake, Charles II, it cost £3,600, but its value was probably six times that sum. Like King Charles's traditional coronet, this circlet bore alternate crosses and fleurs-de-lys spanned by a single arch surmounted by an orb and cross. The gold, reinforced with iridium platinum and studded with seventy-five diamonds and twelve emeralds, possessed a base of ermine and a cap of state of purple velvet in keeping with the mantle. Never before had a coronet or crown been made by electro-forming, a technique of the chemist rather than the old-time practice by which the jeweller-craftsman beat sheets of gold. Briefly, gold was deposited on a wax mould of the coronet, which was immersed in an electro-plating bath for two and a half days. The outcome was a coronet of chemically pure gold, much lighter (weighing only 3 lbs) than a coronet produced by the traditional process.

It was with this coronet that the Queen invested her son. But first the letters patent (which reveal a striking absence of punctuation), by which Charles was created Prince of Wales, were delivered by Garter King of Arms to the Lord Great Chamberlain, who handed them to the Queen. In turn Her Majesty presented them to the Home Secretary, who read:

'Elizabeth the Second by the Grace of God of the United Kingdom of Great Britain and Northern Ireland and of Our other Realms and Territories Queen Head of the Commonwealth Defender of the Faith. To all Lords Spiritual and Temporal and all other Our Subjects whatsoever to whom these Presents shall come Greeting Know Ye that we have made and created and by these Our Letters Do make and create Our most dear Son Charles Philip Arthur George Prince of the United Kingdom of Great Britain and Northern Ireland Duke of Cornwall and Rothesay Earl of Carrick Baron of Renfrew Lord of the Isles and Great Steward of Scotland Prince of Wales and Earl of Chester And to the same Our most dear Son Charles Philip Arthur George have given and granted and by this Our Present Charter Do give grant and confirm the name style title dignity and honour of the same Principality and Earldom And him Our most dear Son Charles Philip Arthur George as he has been accustomed We do ennoble and invest with the said Principality and Earldom by girding him with a Sword by putting a coronet on his head and a Gold Ring on his finger and also by delivering a Gold Rod into his hand that he may preside there and may direct and defend those parts To hold to him and his heirs Kings of the United Kingdom of Great Britain and Northern Ireland and of Our other Realms and Territories Heads of the Commonwealth for ever. Wherefore We will and strictly command for us Our heirs and successors that Our most dear Son Charles Philip Arthur George may have the name style title dignity and honour of the Principality of Wales and Earldom of Chester aforesaid unto him and his heirs Kings of the United Kingdom of Great Britain and Northern Ireland and of Our other Realms and Territories Heads of the Commonwealth as is above mentioned. In Witness whereof We have caused these Our Letters to be made Patent. Witness Ourself at Westminster the twenty-sixth day of July in the seventh year of Our Reign.'

As the Home Secretary read, the Queen invested Prince Charles with the insignia, adjusting the coronet and mantle. Then as the Charter was read again – this time by the Secretary of State for Wales in Welsh – the ceremony reached its moving climax. Kneeling before his mother, the Prince paid homage to the Queen, as, placing his hands between hers, he declared: 'I, Charles, Prince of Wales, do become your liege man of life and limb and of earthly worship, and faith and truth I will bear unto you to live and die against all manner of folks.'

Handing the letters patent to the Prince, the Queen raised him, and after exchanging the Kiss of Fealty, Prince Charles sat on the Queen's right as Sir Ben Bowen Thomas, president of the University College of Wales, read a loyal address in Welsh and English. The Prince replied, also in both languages: 'It is indeed my firm intention to associate myself in word and deed with as much of the life of the Principality as possible.'

In a short religious service, in both languages, there were Bible readings from *I Peter* in English: 'Be subject for the Lord's sake to every human institution, whether it be to the emperor as supreme or to governors as sent by him to punish those who do wrong and to praise those who do right ... Honour all men. Love the brotherhood ... Fear God ... Honour the emperor.' Extracts from *Matthew* were in Welsh, taken from a Bible completed in 1588 by Bishop Morgan: 'Render therefore to Caesar the things that are Caesar's, and to God the things that are God's. When they heard it, they marvelled; and they left Him and went away.' Many consider that the Morgan Bible saved the Welsh language from deteriorating and as such see it as the foremost book in Welsh history. Accompanied by the Duke of Edinburgh, a mere spectator on this occasion, the Queen presented her son to the people of Wales at three points: Queen Eleanor's Gate, overlooking Castle Square; on the steps outside King's Gate, the main entrance to the castle; and the Lower Ward (inside the castle). At each point trumpeters of the Royal Military School of Music sounded a fanfare.

A fly-past by the Royal Air Force formed a spectacular finale as the procession wound back through the streets of Caernarvon. Television had taken the ceremony into 6,350,000 homes; many more people would see edited extracts. At Holyhead the Prince of Wales was the host at a dinner party on the royal yacht *Britannia* that night. The next day he began a four-day tour of his principality. At Glynllifon, once the home of the Newboroughs but now an agricultural college, mishaps marred what was hailed as the ball of the decade: the symbolic daffodils that were expected from the Kenyan village of Molo were never sent because of a surprise drought, and during the first half-hour the ballroom was in darkness when the lights fused through overloading.

Prince Charles's progress – a journey by road in the Queen's maroon Rolls-Royce, a helicopter and the royal yacht – began at Llandudno, where during the night divers searched beneath the pier for bombs. Another probe was conducted among the flowers along the promenade. On that first day the Prince proceeded through the Conway Valley, by Lake Bala to Newport in Montgomeryshire, to New Quay, Cardiganshire and Fishguard. On the second day, after attending divine service at St David's Cathedral, the Prince's party motored in Carmarthenshire and then to Llanelli, Swansea and Moriston. The third day saw the Prince concentrating on the mining areas of the south – Merthyr, Ebbw Vale, Brynmawr, Abertillery, Aberberg and Pontypool, ending at Newport. Each night the party returned to the royal yacht. The Prince's final day was spent at Cardiff, where he met youth representatives in the castle grounds. In the evening he entrained for London.

Apart from the dismantling of a biscuit tin of explosives on a road near Bettws-y-Coed, there had been no cause for alarm. Yet the Russian authorities, perhaps wishing to convince their people of the blessedness of communist life, graphically described on Moscow Radio the holocaust of the houses and cars burning fiercely along the royal route as bombs exploded.

As the letters patent (which are not challengeable in law) indicated, by being created Prince of Wales he had simultaneously acquired the rank of Earl of Chester. The earldom is the most ancient of all the dignities of the heir apparent and relates to the County Palatine of Chester. The word palatine, which is derived from the Latin *palatinus*, was the designation during the later Roman Empire of officials who attended on the emperor or fulfilled duties at his court.

The Normans brought the system to England, where it signified – in the form 'county palatine' – a county of such status that it stood aloof from normal administration. In England the palatine counties faced the country's boundaries with Wales, Scotland and France: Chester, Durham and perhaps Kent.

At the Norman Conquest William the Conqueror created the Chester palatinate for his nephew Hugh, and it remained in his family until 1232, when it was surrendered to the crown. For the next five years the title was held by John le Scot, Earl of Huntingdon, nephew of William the Lion, King of Scotland, and when he died it was annexed to the crown. In 1254 the title was bestowed on Prince Edward, the heir of Henry III, and ten years later, when Simon de Montfort defeated the King at Lewes, Edward suffered the humiliation of resigning his earldom to the Frenchman in exchange for that of Leicester. Resulting from the fluctuations of war, the Chester title reverted to him after the death of de Montfort at Evesham in 1265.

When the Prince succeeded his father as Edward I, he granted the title to Alphonso, his elder son, but on the latter's death when ten years old, the King's second son, who would be known as Edward of Caernarvon, was created the first English Prince of Wales. This was in 1301, when Edward also inherited the Earldom of Chester. An act of 1398, in the reign of Richard II, decreed that it should be granted to the sovereign's eldest son. This law was repealed by Henry IV, but since then the titles of Prince of Wales and Earl of Chester have been conferred jointly on the male heir to the throne. Treated as an ordinary peerage, the Earldom of Chester merges in the crown when the heir apparent ascends to the throne. It is re-created for the next beneficiary.

Because the title of Prince of Wales is not that of a peer, only as Earl of Chester has Prince Charles the right to a seat in the House of Lords. To mark his ennoblement, the Cheshire Community Council presented him with a beautifully bound copy of the *Historical Atlas of Cheshire*.

6 Two Notable Heirs

Prince Charles is the twenty-first Prince of Wales, an honour ranking next to that of the monarch. But how did this title arise?

As John Selden, the seventeenth-century antiquary, explains, it
'was transferred from those Princes of Wales (incidentally, of North
Wales in particular) that, in the elder times being Welsh, held the
country under the Kings of England, by the name of Princes. Neither
was there any other besides them to whom the peculiar Title
of Prince was attributed, as it is a subordinate dignity, Princeps
Walliae and Dominus Snowdoniae, was their usual title.' Yet the
title is both nebulous and meaningless unless we first reflect on
those frenzied times when, despite fierce resistance, the ancient
Britons capitulated to the invading Saxons. Secrets wrested by
archaeological research reveal that at least some, escaping from
the relentless onslaught, fled to the west of Britain.

Ironically, the belligerent tribesmen from northern Germany spoke
contemptuously of the natives as *wealhas*, or strangers, and this
gave Wales and the Welsh their name. They also carved the country
into seven kingdoms – the heptarchy – each striving for supremacy,
the Kings of Northumberland emerging all-powerful for a while.
In retrospect it is clear that King Oswy's shattering defeat of the
Welsh in AD 655 callously ended the aspirations of the old inhabit-
ants to retrieve their country. Sir John Lloyd, in his admirable
History of Wales, claims that Oswy 'was recognised by Saxon,
Angle, Briton, Pict and Scot as the supreme ruler of Britain, and
after his death a good part of his authority was retained by his
son Egfrith'. Yet hope still lingered in many hearts that freedom
would be rekindled when the bones of the fabled seventh-century
Cadwaladr, the 'benign monarch' and monkish recluse in Rome,
were borne from Italy to his native soil.

Meanwhile, the *wealhas*, or Welsh, fought with Saxons and other
intruders. Six centuries would elapse before they submitted to

brutal oppression. Before that, in the eighth century, there were signs that Saxon pressure had begun to ease; Offa, King of Mercia, built his gargantuan dyke or ditch from the Bristol Channel to the Irish Sea, a tangible expression of wisdom that earned the admiration of Charles the Great. Offa's aim was two-fold: henceforth no Welshman was to set foot across the dyke and in return the Welsh would go unmolested.

Offa's successor, Egbert of Wessex, is described in the *Anglo-Saxon Chronicle* as Bretwalada, or Ruler of Britain. But it appears to have been an unstable supremacy, for his grandson, the scholarly Alfred the Great, found himself locked in battle to save Wessex from Viking marauders. In 878, the year when Alfred suppressed the Danes, there died in Wales a man named Rhodri Mawr, who had united the Welsh. Unfortunately custom eroded all that Rhodri had accomplished, for by the Welsh law of inheritance his realm was divided among six sons. No longer boasting of a single king, Wales now had six ruling princes, all paying homage to King Alfred, the champion of the Christian faith against the pagan Danes.

As Sir John Lloyd has commented: 'The basis was laid of the homage which in later ages was regularly demanded from all Welsh princes by the English Crown.' Stubborn refusal to comply would result in the cruel extermination of the Welsh Princes of Wales years hence. By then there would be many princes in Wales. From Anarawd, Rhodri's eldest son, would descend the Princes of Powis, who were to be the last holders of the title of Prince of Wales. Cadell, the second son, would found the line of the ambitious Gruffyd ap Llewellyn, who, acknowledged for a while by all Wales as master, extended his territories with fierce forays over Offa's dyke.

The easy-going Edward the Confessor supinely tolerated his encroachment into Herefordshire and Cheshire, but Gruffyd had not reckoned on Harold, Edward's aggressive henchman, who brooked no humiliation. By brilliant manoeuvring, Harold outmatched Gruffyd in the north and enemies among his own countrymen treacherously hastened his collapse. The head of the last Welsh king was ignominiously conveyed to the triumphant Saxon.

That was in 1063 – three years before Harold, whom history would know as the last Saxon king, himself perished in the fateful clash with the Normans at Hastings. At first his death triggered off rejoicing in Wales, but the jubilation was short-lived; William the

Conqueror would be much more ruthless, not only demanding total obeisance from the Welsh but bringing feudalism from across the English Channel and intending to be the overlord in both Wales and England. The Welsh again resorted to arms.

Despite some Norman encroachment, the Welsh were deeply entrenched in the north – that is, in Gwynedd or Snowdonia – and the centre, leaving Norman footholds in the south and the borderland, known as the Welsh Marches. Not surprisingly, in the south the word 'lord' was substituted for 'prince', but in Snowdonia the title persisted until the thirteenth century, when Welsh independence was gradually snuffed out. But before that day arrived the Welsh would inflict a terrible defeat on their Anglo-Norman foe, in places stamping desolation on the Marches.

Fuller chronicled these sufferings, relating how he was much affected

'... with the ingenuity of an English nobleman who, following the camp of King Henry III in these parts [Caernarvonshire], wrote home to his friends, about the end of September, 1245, the naked truth indeed, as followeth: "We lie in our tents, watching, fasting, praying and freezing. We watch, for fear of the Welshmen, who are wont to invade us in the night; we fast, for want of meat, for the half-penny loaf is worth five-pence; we pray to God to send us home speedily; and we freeze, for want of winter garments, having nothing but thin linen between us and the wind."'

Whenever domestic wrangles harassed the King of England, the Welsh invariably snatched the chance to augment his anxieties or ally with the rebel cause. It was an intolerable situation that reached its peak in the reign of Henry III, when Llewellyn aided the rebel Simon de Montfort, plundering the estates of some Marcher barons. With de Montfort's death the fighting ceased. The subsequent Treaty of Montgomery might have heaped humiliation on the Welsh, yet 'the Lord King of England, wishing to enhance the personal greatness of the said Llewellyn, and in him to honour others who shall succeed him by hereditary right, simply out of his kindness and generosity and with the free will and consent of the Lord Edward, his eldest son, grants to the aforesaid Llewellyn and his heirs the Principality of Wales, and that the same Llewellyn and his heirs shall be called "Princes of Wales".'

All other Welsh princes were to be his vassals. With astonishing lenience, the English allowed Llewellyn to retain much of the land he had conquered, if he paid indemnity and did homage to the English sovereign. Moreover he retained the Four Cantreds, an area stretching from the town of Conway to the River Dee, which the King had previously granted to his heir. In the circumstances, one would have expected Henry's magnanimity to put an end to strife. But peace in those unstable times was fragile, collapsing completely after Henry's death. Crusading in Palestine at the time, Edward I was not crowned until 1274 – two years later. The Prince of Wales was absent; neither had he paid the annual indemnity of 3,000 marks, or rendered homage. The fiery monarch could not ignore such arrogance. In the subsequent conflict the Prince of Wales, beleaguered in his fortress in Snowdonia, was starved into submission. The Treaty of Conway drastically reduced his status. Only five barons were now his vassals, he was deprived of the Cantreds and homage and indemnity could be evaded no longer.

One man made certain that he never forgot. Robert Burnel still recalled the family home at Acton Burnel in Shropshire and the dread when the Welsh were known to be near. Burnel was not only Bishop of Bath and Wells but also the Chancellor of England. When he summoned the Prince to London, Llewellyn appealed to the Church, pleading to be excused because 'the place was not safe, and indifferent for him to appear at'. His request being refused, he offered to journey to Westminster if Burnel would be a hostage at Snowdonia, thus guaranteeing his safe return.

Where anger and cajolery had failed, guile succeeded. De Montfort had promised Llewellyn Eleanor, his daughter, in marriage, but on Simon's death both his widow and daughter had left for Montargis, a nunnery in France. Llewellyn asked for his bride, but on her voyage to Wales some Bristolians, maybe seeking royal favour, captured her off the Scilly Isles and took her to the King. The human bait was irresistible: Llewellyn humbled himself and accepted the King's terms without question.

The outcome was a happy one – at least temporarily. On an autumn morning in 1278, Llewellyn married his bride, whom the King chivalrously gave away. Tragically death would claim Eleanor while giving birth to her daughter Gwenllian, who would live out her life as a nun. Llewellyn himself died in a revolt: perhaps smarting under the royal yoke, in a final bid he had inspired the Welsh to rise. This bid was chronicled by Caradoc of Llangarfan, who describes how

'... the Earl of Gloucester and Sir Edmund Mortimer with an army in South Wales ... there fought with the Prince's friends at Llhandillo Vawhr, and gave them an overthrow ... And all this while the Prince destroyed the country of Cardigan and all the lands of Rees ap Meredith, who served the king in all these wars. But afterwards the Prince separated himself from his army with a few, and came to Buehlt ... and by chance, as he came by the water Wye, there were Edmund Mortimer and John Gifford with great number of soldiers ... Edmund Mortimer's men were of that country, for his father was lord thereof. Then the Prince departed from his men, and went to the valley, with his squire alone, to talk with certain lords of the country who had promised to meet him there.

'Then some of his men ... kept the bridge called the Pont Orewyn, and defended the passage manfully, till they [the enemy] fell upon them ... in their backs, and put them to flight. The Prince's esquire told the Prince ... and as he would have escaped to his men [the enemy] pursued him so hard that one Adam Francton ran him through ... Francton went to despoil him whom he had slain; and when he saw his face he knew him very well, and stroke off his head, and sent it to the King at the Abbey of Conway, who received it with great joy and caused it to be set upon one of the highest turrets of the Tower of London. This was the end of Llewellyn, betrayed by the men of Buehlt, who was the last Prince of Briton's blood who bore dominion and rule in Wales.'

In his history of England Carte relates how the Prince, who had died unrepentant, lay rotting for some time uninterred. Then, whether truthfully or not, someone claimed that he had heard the Prince ask for a priest in his dying moments. A charitable Archbishop of Canterbury granted absolution and the last of the British princes of the blood of Cadwaladr the Blessed was given fitting burial. Llewellyn left no heir. His brother David, who had enjoyed English friendship before he rebelled, had been tortured to death.

Edward began to annex North Wales with England, but the process was complex and slow; Welsh law and local government had to be replaced by English counterparts amid smouldering resentment. To preserve the peace Edward began to build a chain of fortresses, but his conquest over Welsh intransigence had left him with a tremendous task. He was still at Rhuddlan when, in the spring of 1284, a messenger bore the news that his consort, Eleanor of Castile, had given birth to a son. The date was 25 April – St Mark's Day. Eleanor was also in Wales, housed in temporary accommodation at Caernarvon, where a massive castle and town were rising, replacing the Norman 'motte and bailey'. A document in Westminster Abbey records the event: 'In the year 1284, on the day of St Mark the

Evangelist, at Caernarvon in Snowdonia, there was born to the King a son, who was named Edward and at whose birth many rejoiced, especially the Londoners.' He was the first of two notable heirs (the other being the Black Prince) who would between them receive the major English titles that would pass centuries later to Prince Charles.

At Caernarvon he conferred the first English charter of rights and privileges granted in Wales. Edward had good reason to rejoice: his first two sons were dead and the eleven-year-old Alphonso, the heir apparent, was a weakling due for an early demise. Legend claims that the King, honouring his pledge to provide the turbulent Welsh barons with a prince 'that was borne in Wales and could speake never a word of English', presented his newborn son to them. 'Here is your man,' he is said to have cried. Phil Morris RA has depicted this scene on canvas, but it is held to be apocryphal. It was first recorded in the days of the first Elizabeth, and John Stow gave it credence in his *Annales of England*. Doubtless Edward was ready to resort to any ploy that would help him to unite Britain, but surely such a gesture would have grossly insulted the Welsh smouldering under defeat. And to honour the second son rather than the heir apparent is inconceivable. Legend, therefore, is eclipsed by fact. For instance a room in the Eagle Tower is traditionally the scene of Edward's gesture, but at that time the tower's construction was still in its early stages.

However the grandiose christening of Edward of Caernarvon, as a manuscript presented to the British Museum conveys, was unique in the munificence shown to the officiating cleric, Anan, Bishop of Bangor. The King awarded him with manors and regalities in Anglesey and Caernarvon and the ferries of Borthnan and Cadnant over the Menai.

When Edward was four months old Alphonso died, making the baby prince the heir apparent. By now he had left Wales, and he had attained manhood before he saw the principality again. In his childhood Edward was never over-endowed with parental love. In his sixth year his mother died and marriage for three sisters would deprive him of their companionship too. As for the King, he was forty-five years the boy's senior, and the age gap was doubtless widened by rigid discipline. As with some other princes, it was to his nurses that Edward turned for affection and in return they won his lasting regard. Thought for those who tended them in infancy is a trait common to many princes. Prince Charles himself is included in this category, though he did not have to struggle through such a disturbed childhood, which included illness. When Edward suffered 'a spasm in the stomach' his weight in wax candles was offered at the nearest shrine. When smallpox assailed him, his doctor ordered that he should be 'enveloped in scarlet cloth, and that his bed and all the furniture of his chamber should be of a bright-red colour'.

Edward's favourite home was the royal manor of Langley in Hertfordshire, where, to the contempt and dismay of many contemporaries, he indulged in rural activity: thatching and ditching, working with the blacksmith at the forge and drinking ale with common folk such as carters and household servants. A writer of those days complained with some asperity that if the Prince 'had given to arms the labour that he expended on rustic pursuits, he would have raised England aloft'. In our own times it is placed to his credit when Queen Elizabeth II says of the Prince of Wales: 'He is like the rest of our family; we are all country people.' For some years Edward shared with his five older sisters a royal household that – as is illustrated by a housekeeping account – was costly to maintain. In 1289, for instance, when the Prince was five years old, the bill, excluding wines, totalled some £2,140, a substantial sum in the thirteenth century. No doubt to his displeasure the young prince lost the camaraderie of his sisters when not quite thirteen, and now about to be 'brought into greater prominence and to assume, at any rate in name, certain public responsibilities, he received a household of his own'.

At about this time, though still a boy, Edward savoured his first taste of state affairs, which he grew to dislike. On a Sunday in July 1297, when he was about to engage in a bitter war with Philip IV of France, the King appealed to the people assembled outside Westminster Hall. At his side on the dais stood his eldest son. 'Behold,' cried the King, according to a contemporary record, 'I am about to expose myself to danger on your account. I pray you, if I return, receive me as you have at present. But if I do not return, crown my son as your King.' The chronicler adds that 'all the magnates there present did fealty to the King's son at his father's bidding, and he was acclaimed by all the people, their right hands upraised, as heir ... and successor to the kingdom.' His appointment as guardian of the realm was nominal, for the task of government was entrusted to the King's Council. Yet during his regency of seven months, an incident occurred that drastically changed the course of English history. Although the people groaned beneath swingeing taxation, the cunning Edward I had ordered a further levy, hoping that his son's popularity would induce the people to accept the burden. But London's enraged citizens rebelled, demanding exemption from all taxation, save by their own consent or agreed by themselves or their representatives. So great was the outcry that Edward of Caernarvon was forced to sanction the enactment that 'no tax henceforth be levied or laid by us [the King] or our heirs, in this our realm without the good will and common assent of the archbishop, bishops and other prelates, the earls, barons, knights, burgesses, and other freemen of our realm'.

Thus a vital clause that led to democratic freedom – a clause that was a dead letter in the Magna Carta of King John, and was cunningly omitted from that of Henry III – was restored by the first Prince of Wales of English blood. From now on Parliament's control of the public purse would be the instrument that, down the centuries, would slowly denude the sovereigns of their ancient powers, leaving Britain with a constitutional or limited monarchy, to which Prince Charles will eventually aspire.

To revert to Prince Edward, it may be that the domestic cleavage – the separation from sisterly love – set the pattern for the fateful course of Edward's life. Closest to him in age and affection was Elizabeth, but it was Joan, born at Acre during a crusade and a girl of resolute mind, who might have bolstered his character and spared him the tragedy that lay ahead. Unfortunate traits would reveal themselves. But meanwhile Edward grew into a 'well proportioned and handsome person, of a courteous disposition and well-bred', and 'managed his steed wonderfully well'. Sir Guy Ferre, a soldier and courtier of considerable experience, was appointed the prince's tutor and guardian. But he failed to foster interest in knightly exercises – the basic requirement for a medieval aristocrat – or in learning. He lacked enthusiasm and was bored to distraction by whatever training he received for kingship. He normally spoke in Norman French, but a prince of those times needed some knowledge of English – if only to converse with humbler subjects – and Latin, then the *lingua franca* of European diplomacy.

Everything implies that Edward was no scholar, but this has never been a rudiment of kingship. Against this was his love of certain

arts: architecture, the theatre and music. His patronage was extended at all times to musicians and minstrels, and he tried to
foster interest in a type of violin known by Welsh exponents
as the *crwth*. It is on record that he summoned a *croudarius* to
perform at Windsor Castle, rewarded Richard le Croudere for entertaining both himself and his sister Elizabeth, and dispatched Richard
the Rhymer, a member of his household, to study the instrument at
Shrewsbury. The feudal lords eyed with distaste the Prince's predilection for theatricals and buffoonery. And after his accession
many scorned the appointment as treasurer of England of Walter
Reynaud, whose attributes were confined to stage production and
acting.

In the Middle Ages such aesthetic tastes were interpreted as
effeminacy. In Prince Edward's case the accusation was not unfounded. While he was in Flanders during the war, a man called
Piers de Gaveston, son of Arnaud de Gaveston, a Gascon knight
who had served the King, had been recruited as squire in the
royal household. When the King returned to England Piers came
too, to become one of the ten companions in Prince Edward's household. The presence of Piers at Court proved disastrous. As an
anonymous writer recorded three decades later: 'When the King's
son saw him he fell so much in love that he entered upon an en-
during compact with him.' Wrongly accused by his enemies of being
the son of a witch burnt at Guyenne, Piers – arrogant, cultivated,
intelligent and vicious – nurtured the homosexual proclivities of the
heir apparent. 'Faire of body and grate of strengthe' – that sum-
marizes the outward appearance of this Plantagenet prince. But he
was manifestly weak in character – malleable material in the hands
of the evil Gascon. Both would indulge in dissolute pleasures, the
more crafty intellect domineering and shaping the feckless mind.
Without doubt Gaveston led the first English Prince of Wales along
paths of sin, bred between monarch and son an enmity that at times
reached fearful proportions, and set patron and servant on the
dangerous course that brought savage death to both.

It has been said that this passion for 'Brother Gaveston' matured
when, experiencing the heat of battle for the first time, the Prince
aided his father in the war with the Scots. During a lull in hostilities,
the King summoned a Parliament at Lincoln, there raising his son
– who had already inherited the Duchy of Aquitaine and the lordship of Ponthieu – to the dignity of Prince of Wales and investing

him with all the royal lands in the principality. These embraced all North Wales, stretching from Chester to the estuary of the Dyfi, Anglesey, Snowdonia and those territories now named Cardiganshire, with all rights, privileges and profits, including wrecks at sea. Also bestowed on him was the earldom of Chester, from which he derived castles and manors, not only in the palatinate but scattered about England. The charter was dated 7 February 1301, yet, curiously, nowhere does the title of Prince appear.

Now officially Llewellyn's successor, Edward set off to receive Welsh homage. The people, 'esteeming him their rightful lord, because he derived his origin from those parts', acclaimed him. But perhaps his greatest joy lay in the musicality of the Welsh.

Edward was known as Prince of Wales for the first time on 10 May 1301, when a further legal deed gave him more territory and placed the principality under his government. Then in April 1302 the manor of Langley, the scene of so much childhood happiness, was also granted to him on the death of Edmund, Earl of Cornwall. Thus from the age of seventeen Edward of Caernarvon bore the title of Prince of Wales. Until the King's death there would be intermittent quarrels between father and son, the worst erupting when the perverted Prince foolishly tried to give his inheritance of Ponthieu to Gaveston. The ungovernable Plantagenet wrath could not be curbed. 'Thou to give away lands,' cried the furious King. 'Thou who never won any! God alive! Were it not that the kingdom might fall into anarchy I would take good care that thou wouldst never come to thine inheritance!' In his frenzy he snatched his son by the hair and, it is recorded, extracted it by the handful.

'Perot' – little Peter – as the Prince called his favourite, was banished for life, but on the death of the old sovereign, his heir – now Edward II – recalled him, making him regent in his absence while he crossed the Channel to marry Isabella, the daughter of Philip of France. From the outset the union was doomed: the King preferred the couch of Gaveston to that of the Queen, so that 'she saw the King a stranger to her bed, and revelling in the embraces of his wanton minions, without so much as a glance or look on her deserving beauty'. Not until Gaveston's deplorable death in May 1312 at Blacklaw Hill near Warwick did Isabella bear children. A caucus of insurgent barons led by the King's cousin, the Earl of Lancaster, put an end to the hated Gascon. A Welsh soldier skewered him with his sword while another callously sliced off his head. In a sense, by his perverted ways the first Prince of Wales was the cause of frightful repercussions, for those fateful strokes of the sword introduced two centuries of baronial conflict. As for the King, the penalty for humiliating his embittered consort was inexorable. To Edward, who 'carried a knife in his hose to kill Queen Isabella, and had said that if he had no other weapon he would crush her with his teeth', his consort – 'the she-wolf of France' – was henceforth his relentless foe. Edward was captured while fleeing to Wales. Parliament demanded his abdication, so that the first English Prince of Wales was also the first English monarch to be deposed. And while the ousted sovereign was held prisoner, Isabella – 'one of the feyrest ladyes of the worlde' – demeaned herself by acquiescing in the heinous crime of her paramour, Roger Mortimer. On a September night in 1327, at Berkeley Castle, her avengers 'took him [the King] in his bed, and casting heavy bolsters upon him, and pressing him down, stifled him; and not content with that, they heated an iron red hot, and through a pipe thrust it up into his fundament, that no marks of violence might be seen; but though none were seen, yet some were heard, for when the fact was in doing, he was heard to roar and cry all the castle over.'

At first it seems odd that since the time of Edward of Caernarvon – a period of some seven centuries – there have been a mere twenty Princes of Wales. Through tortuous history we arrive at Prince Charles. Yet only by accidents of fate is he heir to the throne. Moreover, but for the deaths of two Princes of Wales, England's historical scene would have changed vastly. After the slaughter at Bosworth, Lord Stanley took the crown from a bush and placed it on the head of Henry Tudor, Earl of Richmond. To some extent the old prophecy of Cadwaladr, the last King of the Britons, that his people would regain their native land was now in effect reality. The thrifty Welshman, who never forgot his parsimonious past, was now King of England, to be known as Henry VII. His claim to the throne was tenuous. No one could dispute his descent from Edward II, but he did so through the illegitimate offspring of John of Gaunt. These children had since been legitimized, but Henry's strongest claim to the crown lay in his marriage to Elizabeth, the indisputable heiress among the Yorkist faction. Henry, sensitive to the smear on his pedigree, sent commissioners into Wales to trace his forebears.

It does not seem an accident that he christened his elder son Arthur. The name revived the glory of the Arthurian legends, which, with their patriotic tales of European conquest, would excite the hearts of Welshmen, and not a few in England too. Much was expected from Prince Arthur: he would rekindle the flame of his immortal namesake. But the lustre faded; Arthur lay dead before his sixteenth birthday. One wonders what England's destiny would have been in an Arthurian era. We shall never know; instead the throne was occupied by the burly and ebullient prince who became Henry VIII.

There is a parallel in the story of Henry of Stirling, the first son of the garrulous James I. Henry, a brilliant youth who was loved both for himself and for his skills, seemed assured of a reign that would benefit king and country alike. Of enormous potential, Henry was markedly different from his father and his younger brother Charles. He was not, for instance, obsessed by his father's calamitous doctrine of the divine right of kings, which bedevilled the Stuart reigns. In various ways, although on the surface he was obedient to the King, his convictions tended to stem from his own views and not from those of his father. It is possible that with Henry of Stirling on the throne, the seeds of strife, resulting in the growing conflict between King and Parliament, would never have been sown or, if they had, would have been amiably resolved. But Henry was dead at nineteen, to be succeeded by his melancholy brother Charles, whose stubbornness both in religion and in politics helped to breed Cromwell's Commonwealth no less than Puritan bigotry.

Even if one dismisses both Arthur and Henry, but for the political machinations of the Whigs, the status of Prince Charles could never have been what it is today. For the Whigs, rightly or wrongly, snatched from the Stuarts their hereditary right, and in what has been dubbed the Glorious Revolution purged the nation of papist monarchs, replacing them with Protestant Hanoverians and the House of Windsor.

Of all the twenty-one English Princes of Wales eleven have been the offspring of sovereigns, and twelve have occupied the throne. Yet there were moments when the crown seemed beyond the reach of some. One example is Edward of the Sanctuary, so named because he entered this world in the sanctuary of Westminster after his father, Edward IV, had fled his realm. The Queen and her son relied solely on charity. Henry of Monmouth, subsequently known as Henry v, seemed so remote from the crown that £2 was considered to be an adequate fee for the 'wise woman' who attended his birth. The crown completely evaded James Francis Edward Stuart. Unconscious of the political ferment that drove his father to flight, the baby prince was borne away to live and die in exile.

Only fourteen Princes of Wales were actually born in England, and until the birth of the future Edward VIII not one had been born in England of English-born parents since the union of Henry VII and Elizabeth of York some four centuries earlier. One Prince of Wales was born in Bordeaux, two were born in Scotland and two in Hanover, but only two were born in the principality itself.

The second Prince of Wales, Edward of Woodstock, victor of Crécy and Poitiers (who came to be known as the Black Prince years after his death), never succeeded his father Edward III. Yet he is of unusual significance in that the main titles and dignities possessed by Prince Charles originated in his lifetime. In an age when grandiose pomp and materialism were rife, Edward III lavished riches on his 'fair, lusty and well-formed' son. The Prince was only three when he was belted Earl of Chester; for the 'sustenance' of the newly created peer Philippa, the King's consort, received an annual rent of 500 marks from the 'profits' of that city. With the earldom went four castles and numerous revenues from the Cantreds. Four years later the young prince was elevated to a much higher distinction. The King's brother, John of Eltham, Earl of Cornwall, had died without heirs and the young Edward received Cornwall – now raised to a dukedom – as well. In this manner the Duchy of Cornwall was instituted and the title of 'duke' – not unknown on the Continent – made its initial appearance in the history of England. Henceforth the dignity would assure the livelihood of 'the oldest sons of his heirs, Kings of England'. Not all the castles and manors were confined to Cornwall and over the centuries other estates were absorbed, the whole ensuring the income of successive heirs apparent.

War had again erupted, because Edward III was claiming the French crown by right of Isabella, his mother. To secure an alliance with the Flemings, he had assumed the title of the French king at Ghent, and now the arms of France were quartered with those of England, remaining there until George III discreetly removed them four centuries later. Having struck the first blows in what would burgeon into the Hundred Years' War, he temporarily returned to England, with the words *Dieu et mon Droit* (God and my right) emblazoned as his motto – the motto of British monarchs to this day. One of his first acts was to summon a Parliament at Westminster to create the Duke of Cornwall – not yet thirteen – the second Prince of Wales. The event was celebrated with jousts at Smithfield for three days – 'and the challengers came forth, one apparelled like to the Pope, bringing with him twelve others in garments like to Cardinals'. Among the defenders was the recently created Prince of Wales. To highlight this knightly ardour an invitation was issued throughout Europe to those 'renowned for virtue and valour' to participate in a feast of the Round Table eulogizing the immortal King Arthur. We read that the festival gave an impetus to trade and that 'the King's tailors were kept busy making robes, hosen, coverchiefs, with super-tunic for his majesty at a cost of 14s.'. Intending to hold these festivities annually, the King ordered the construction of the Round Tower at Windsor on what tradition claimed to be the site of King Arthur's table. For a while, however, chivalrous jollifications had to be postponed: the rancour between Philip of France and Edward of England was smouldering again. The truce was broken and at last the controversy was to be settled 'by battle or an honourable peace'.

The Prince of Wales, now sixteen, was also to savour the rank taste of war. In the clash of arms he would win his spurs on an August day at Crécy. Among the dead lay the old blind King of Bohemia, with his crest of an eagle's wing and motto *Ich dien* (I serve). Tradition asserts that, adapting this motto, the young Edward devised from the eagle's wing his personal crest of ostrich feathers, creating the crest of England's Prince of Wales since that gory day in 1346. The tale makes for romance; indeed it is almost sacrosanct in English history. More recent historians, however, have irreligiously cast doubts on its authenticity. William Camden, in his *Remaines*, is credited with having divulged the story. In his original account he gave Poitiers as the scene where the Black Prince secured the crest, but eventually changed it to Crécy. Camden quotes no source for his account, yet a treatise on medicine, written in Latin, which was contemporaneous with the Black Prince, specifically describes the incident. The author, John Arderne, a leech in the employ of Edward III, accompanied the English forces to France. His services were so admired by the Prince's retinue that he was awarded a grant of land in Ireland. Copies were made of Arderne's manuscript, but not all contained the account. The one in which it did appear devoted a section to haemorrhoids. Arderne revealed: 'And it should be observed that such a white feather was borne by Edward the eldest son of Edward King of England above his crest, and that he won the feather from the king of Bohemia whom he slew at Crécy in France, and thus took to himself the feather, which is called *Ostrich Fether*, which that most noble king had borne on his crest.' The manuscript, as explained by Arderne, was written in 1376, and on this Sir Harris Nicholas, the antiquarian, has remarked:

'There is therefore undoubtedly the statement of a contemporary who from his situation was likely to be well informed on the subject that the Black Prince took the Ostrich Feather from the crest of the King of Bohemia, whom he slew at Crécy, and assumed it for his own crest; but, though this assertion is entitled to great weight, I am not, I confess, convinced of its accuracy; and I still expect that proof will some day be found that the Ostrich Feather and the mottoes 'Ich Dien' and 'Houmont' were derived from the Prince's maternal house of Hainault [Queen Philippa, the mother of the Black Prince, was a descendant of the Courts of Hainault, on whose escutcheon plumes were emblazoned].'

It should be appreciated that the plume of ostrich feathers, which to most is synonymous with the title, has in fact been the badge of heirs apparent – as distinct from Princes of Wales – since the days of the Tudors. There is no unanimity of opinion as to the accuracy of the motto *Ich Dien* (I serve), either. One school of thought argues that it should be *Eich Dyn* (Your man) – words associated with Edward I when, addressing the Welsh barons, he presented to them his baby son.

During the rapturous aftermath of war the King founded at Windsor the 'Knights of the Blew-Garter'. A companionship of like character had existed before, for had not the first Richard tied a thong round the knees of certain knights to 'signify a union of military qualities'? The King now 'assembled together erles, lordes and knyghtes of the realme and showed them his intecyon, they entertained the notion with great joy and applause considering that it would prove a very great advancement to pietie and nobilitie and virtue, and likewise be an excellent expedient for the uniting not only of his natives one with another, but of foreigners with them in Bonds of Amitye and Peace.'

In the richly colourful scene there was selected 'a certayne nombre of the most valyantest men of the realme, and they sware and sayled to mentayne the ordynaunces such as wer descryed'. Paramount was the rule that knights should 'never turn their back or run away out of the field in time of battell where there is present their sovereign lord' or his deputy or banner. Robes and mantles were to be exactly alike, 'thereby intimating that they should all conserve brotherly love among themselves ... and lest at any time there should be a falling out of the least breath of amitie was the great collar of the order ordained ... in witness of the bond of faythe, peace and amitie strictly to be observed between the Companions each of whom upon election was called upon to produce a sum of money according to his quality and degree'. The King subscribed the most – precisely £26 13s 1d; the contribution of a 'stranger king' was assessed at £20; the Prince of Wales paid £13 6s 8d and mere knights £3 6s 8d. The money was put to a worthy purpose – to 'the relief of the Canons of Windsor' and impoverished knights.

The Order of the Garter, the supreme fraternity among all English honours, would be dedicated to St George, patron of England, and each knight would receive a stall in the magnificent Chapel of St George, which would rise in the next century. Of the founder-knights four, among them the Prince of Wales, were as yet not aged twenty; ten were under thirty and the sovereign himself was only thirty-five. There is speculation that these pioneer companions were the contestants at a spectacular tournament at which the King opposed the Prince of Wales, each backed by a team of twelve. Whether this is true or not, at the Order's annual ceremony in April, the monarch and twelve knights occupy stalls on the south side of the chapel, with the Prince of Wales and twelve more companions on the north. The statutes certainly restrict the knights to twenty-four, augmented by the reigning monarch and the Prince of Wales, each a constituent part of the Order. Long after the Order's inception a story prevailed as to the origin of its motto *Honi soit qui mal y pense* (shamed be he who thinks evil of it). According to one writer, it was first noted in an 'idle romance published by a stranger to the affairs of England and by him taken on no better ground than the tradition of the common people – too trifling evidence to so great a building, common bruit being so infamous an historian that wise men neither report nor give credit to any information they receive from it'.

The story centres on a lady who accidentally dropped her garter. Some attribute this to Queen Philippa herself, others to the Countess of Salisbury. But even here there were conflicting views, for one version claimed that the words were the Queen's retort when the King asked 'what men would conjecture of her upon losing her garter'. Another puts the words in the mouth of the King, who displeased the Queen on picking up this trifle. The most persistent account describes how, with the garter in his hand, he had seen courtiers smile 'as at an amorous act', whereupon he cried: 'You make but small account of this garter, but within a few months I will cause the best of you all to reverence the like.' With this he put the garter round his own leg and uttered the motto. For years the garter story was treated as fiction – the fabrication, so it was thought, of a subsequent age – yet modern research gives the tale some credence. But the lady in question was more likely to be Joan, Countess of Kent, who eventually married the Prince of Wales. The setting of the incident may have been a court ball in Calais, to which Countess Joan accompanied the Queen during the siege.

Of all England's Princes of Wales, by far the greatest aura of romance centres around Edward, the Black Prince. His body was tortured by dropsy and his death preceded that of the King, yet a link with that 'Flower of all the Chivalry in the world at that time' lingers on into modern times. For his victory at Najera in Spain the Prince, so tradition asserts, received a ruby from the hands of Pedro the Cruel, King of Castile. The Black Prince probably wore it on his helmet in battle. It adorned the coronet surrounding the helmet of Henry V at Agincourt. Henry VIII added it to the crown jewels, and as such it may have been the 'rock ruby' sold for £15 during the Commonwealth to a Mr Cook. If that is so, the jewel returned to royal possession – to dominate the imperial state crown that Prince Charles will wear on his accession.

7 Past Princes of Wales

As its basic motif, the pattern of training of Prince Charles has been designed to equip him for monarchical duties in the context of the requirements of his own times. This motif has crystallized the aim of the education of past Princes of Wales. Yet it is surprising how, in many cases, it fell short of its objective. The quality of training – together with the traits and character of the title-holder – often left its impression on history.

Had Prince Charles lived in feudal times his education, like that of other aristocratic sons, would have adhered to a conventional pattern. John Hardyng (1378–1465) left to posterity the medieval curriculum : learning to read from the age of four, studying languages and the finer aspects of breeding at six, and being taught to dance, sing and 'speke of gentelnesse' at ten. By the time he was fourteen a 'lordes sonne' should be sufficiently adept in horsemanship to 'hunte the dere', for within another two years it was necessary to be competent to joust 'and castels to assayle'. In short, the young nobleman, after a degree of learning, was trained for war. Indeed some of England's heirs apparent were seasoned warriors in their adolescence. It was the practice, too, to attach the sons of sovereigns to the households of prominent noblemen for training in those medieval essentials – virtue and chivalry. In England the last prince to be so placed – with the family of Richard Neville, Earl of Warwick – was the future Richard III, whom history suspects of engineering the deaths of the young Princes in the Tower – England's sixth Prince of Wales, the uncrowned Edward V, and his brother Richard of York. In Scotland James VI (later James I of England), already a monarch in his rickety childhood, was groomed by the Earl of Mar.

Since then there emerged the routine by which tutors were employed to educate royal children in their homes. The degree of success of this system has varied enormously, especially as, over the years, the apprenticeship of heirs to the throne has grown progressively more exacting. The education of the two Tudor Princes of Wales, who felt the sharp impact of the Renaissance, confirms this. It was thought essential for young aristocracy to acquire all manner of knowledge, yet still be competent in physical pastimes. The stress was very great and some wilted under it.

Arthur of Winchester, a prince of frail physique, was a notable instance and it is widely believed that a factor in his sudden death was excessive study. His father knighted him and added the dignity of Prince of Wales after his third birthday, and then his lessons began. One gleans from his earliest tutor, an Italian named Friar Bernard Andreas, that he either 'learned without book' or 'studiously learned and revolved with his own hands and eyes' such authors as Homer, Virgil, Caesar, Livy, Lucan, Terence, Pliny, Cicero, Plautus, Sallust, Ovid, Eusebius and Quintilian. This forbidding academic fare was then 'thought fit for the *elementary* and *rudimentary* instruction of princes'. The boy-Prince, a fine Latinist, was so avid for knowledge that the King engaged a second tutor, Dr Thomas Linacre, an eminent scholar and scientist, who founded the Royal College of Physicians. A native of Kent, though of a Derbyshire family, this Fellow of All Souls, Oxford, had studied in Italy where, esteemed at the court of Lorenzo de Medici, he had perfected his knowledge of Greek, medical science and philosophy. The King now entrusted this formidable scholar with 'the task of making the mind and body of Prince Arthur grow in wholesome vigour'.

When he was ten the studious Prince spent two short periods at Oxford's Magdalen College, where he was seen to be more 'in the grave than in the gay aspect of youth'. Pastimes did not have the same appeal. Apparently he showed scant enthusiasm for riding, tennis or the joust, although physical accomplishments were expected of a royal prince at that time. Sometimes he would pitch his tent, set up his butts and practise archery. As a toxophilite he was so skilful that to be called a 'true Prince Arthur' meant the essence of marksmanship.

Henry of Greenwich, the future Henry VIII, was of sturdier stuff than his elder brother and his prodigious energy and robustness kept pace with the 'hard mental labour' imposed by his scholarly tutors. These included John Skelton, Henry VII's poet laureate, who would boast in later years: 'The honour of England I learned [taught] to spell.' Skelton, who figured so prominently in Henry's training, has been described as accomplishing 'the transition between the old learning of the scholastics and the new culture of the humanists', and hailed in his own time as the greatest poet since Chaucer. To guide his royal charge, he wrote a moral treatise in which he enjoined his pupil to 'cultivate sobriety and self-restraint. Avoid drunkenness. Eschew luxury. Shun the company of lewd women. Defile not your marriage' – gentle counsel that Henry blatantly ignored.

Fluent in Italian, Spanish and French, Henry's Latin drew the plaudits even of Erasmus when that great scholar and philosopher, visiting the royal manor at Eltham, was presented to the Prince. The boy, then nine years old, begged to be allowed to correspond with him and Erasmus agreed, 'with ill-concealed pride'. Henry had been subjected to pressures from infancy and faced every new challenge with zest. We see the exuberant little Prince at the age of four astride his pony, trotting through the City to Mile End, anxious to witness a tourney and pit his skill at the butts. In due course he would be a devotee of both tilting and the tournament, but music would claim his attention just as much. Indebted to his mother for his musical skill, he played the organ and the recorder and 'like Luther, Henry, when fatigued with his studies, used to amuse himself by playing on the flute'.

It is on record that the King, having meticulously chosen the Prince's teachers, 'bade them ground the babe well in theology, language and all such learning as would fit him to become Archbishop of Canterbury'. Historians debate this tale among themselves, but a contemporary biographer baldly asserts that the tuition of this talented Prince 'was entirely clerical. He commenced chanting at seven, at ten he had his part assigned him in the choir 'of the Chapel Royal, and at twelve composed masses'. Perhaps there is an element of truth in this and Henry was, until his brother's death, destined for high office in the Church, even with his eyes on the papal throne. Certainly the suggestion must not be summarily dismissed, for Henry was attracted to the Church. Evidence abounds to confirm his love of religious services; indeed he frequently attended five masses in one day. Moreover his study of theology must have been profound, for by all accounts he was 'perilous to all adversaries who ventured to break a lance with him in a theological quarrel'. Only with mature knowledge could he have defended the Catholic Church from Lutheran attack, winning a Pope's gratitude and the title 'Defender of the Faith' – a title that has been bestowed on English monarchs ever since. There is also the view of the King to consider. Henry VII was an astute sovereign and in precarious times he would have profited by having a son as a prince of the Church; if the Prince had worn the papal tiara, the gain to the English throne would have been gargantuan.

Skelton's humanism was flourishing when Henry of Greenwich, now on the throne as Henry VIII, planned the education of his own children. Greek and Latin were then the basic ingredients of the educational diet. His daughters, the half-sisters Mary (later Mary I) and Elizabeth (to be called the Virgin Queen), had tutors at the age of four. The Catholic Catherine of Aragon induced Luis Vives, an eminent theorist on education, to leave his native Spain to teach her daughter, Mary. As a fellow of Corpus Christi College, Vives introduced Greek learning to Oxford and wrote studies in Latin specifically on female education. Even when she was twenty, Mary was devoting her day to the scriptures, languages and music. Though her scholarly achievements were immense, they were far excelled by Elizabeth and by Prince Edward. In the main, their tutors were men of great intellectual capacity at Cambridge, among them Roger Ascham, the calligrapher, and John Cheke, Regius Professor of Greek. Others taught modern languages and arts. Their labours were rewarded: Elizabeth could speak extempore in Latin when replying to formal speeches and address ambassadors from France, Italy and Spain in their native tongues.

Edward attained the crown when he was ten years old, but he lay dead – the victim of a 'tough, strong straining cough' – six years later. Yet in that brief life, dogged by ill-health, he had come to be known as an infant prodigy. In those eventful years of religious strife, when men like Cheke were imbued with reforming zeal, Edward absorbed the new Protestant dogmas written in the tedious Latin of the German theologian Melanchthon.

In the century that separated the Tudor and Stuart Princes of Wales much happened in England. Primarily, religion had changed: the old Catholicism had ceded to the new Protestant faith. Now, to be known as a papist was to evoke abuse, for Protestantism had infected not one isolated section of society, but most of the people, and in its severest form – Puritanism. Not until the nation had grown weary of Puritan harshness during the Commonwealth would many again seek the benevolence and ritual of the Episcopal Church. But the Bible stayed unchallenged, overriding the dictates of the priest and his confessional, so that men were now in direct communion with God, rather than communing with him through the medium of the saints. In such circumstances, only a Protestant could occupy the throne.

Society, too, had been transformed. In place of the ancient aristocracy, which had massacred itself in the insensate Wars of the Roses, a new nobility had arisen, for the most part occupying the monastic lands bought from Henry VIII. The threats and dangers from outside, and their obligation to the Tudors, had caused them to submit to autocratic rule. But those times were past. Under the Stuarts they were to exert their authority through the instrument of Parliament. The early Stuart kings seemed to be oblivious to this, a blind spot that is particularly surprising in the case of James I. He harangued his Parliaments as Elizabeth I had never dared to do. Neither he nor his son Charles appeared to be alert to the prevailing social and political atmosphere; each was obsessed with James's theory of the divine right of kings, a fetish that, coupled with a refusal to move with the religious currents, eventually cost the dynasty the crown.

The type of tuition James arranged for his sons did not help. Both were reared in the traditional manner of Renaissance princes: languages (both dead and living), music and the arts, archery, the wearing of armour and the joust and theology. But James never taught them how to deal with political change. Patronage – a system practised extensively by the Tudors – was on the wane; the new affluent, intent on asserting themselves in state affairs, were not for hire. James failed to inculcate into his sons the need to compromise.

In every other way, the King taxed his sons severely when drawing up their curriculum. It was an echo of his own boyhood, which would have crushed a less robust child by the sheer weight of learning involved. Led by the redoubtable George Buchanan, a Latinist of European fame, a corps of tutors, including musicians and riding masters, laboured with their charge (from the age of four) for some twelve hours daily. 'They gar me speik Latin ar I could speik Scottis,' commented James on this regimen. Peter Young, who had been educated in Calvin's Geneva, cleansed the boy's mind of any possible Popish tendencies and probably invested him with his extensive knowledge of modern history.

This persistent cramming led to setbacks: later James rejected many of his teachers' dictums, among them the austerities of Calvin Presbyterianism. He had grown up as virtually the ward of the Presbyterian Church. Described as 'God's silly vassal', he was determinedly episcopalian when in England, arguing: 'No bishop, no king.' He convinced himself that monarchs were 'justly called gods because they exercise a manner of resemblance to Divine power on earth ... They have power to exalt low things and abase high things and to make of their subjects like men at chess.' This attitude was apparent in the manual – the *Basilikon Doron* ('Kingly Gift') – on kingship, which he composed 'for the special benefit of my deare sonne Henry, appointed by God (I hope) to sit upon the throne'. This monarch, who gave his patronage to Shakespeare, and was a poet of modest attainment himself, wrote his preface in verse:

> It should be your chief and princlie care
> To follow virtue, vice for to forbeare.
>   Your father bids you studie here and redde,
>   How to be a perfect King indeed!

The manual is divided into three parts, the first being a discourse 'Anent the King's Christian Duty Towards God'; the second deals with 'A King's Duty in His Office'; and the third, 'Anent a King's Behaviour in Indifferent Things', concerns such matters as table manners. Henry was only a boy at the time, but he was deemed to be intelligent enough to cope with the King's pedantic precepts and doctrines. James listed 'Justice, Clemency, Magnanimity, Liberality, Constancy, and Humility' as the princely virtues most likely to make for sound kingship, and enlightened the Prince on his twofold debt to God: 'First because he made you a man and next for that he made you a little God to sit on his throne and rule over other men ... The whole Scripture consisteth of two things, a command and a prohibition – to do such things and to abstain from the contrarie. Obey in both, nor think it enough to abstain from evil and do no good ... Keep God sparingly in your mouth but abundantlie in your heart.' For the Prince to honour his parents was essential: 'I grant ye we have our faults which (privately betwixt you and God) should serve ye for examples to meditate upon and mend in your own person, but should not be a matter of discourse to others.'

Kingly character also guaranteed that the law was obeyed by the nobility as well as by the humblest. The Prince must protect the poor and appreciate that when he sat in judgement he was sitting on God's throne, and must not be diverted from what was right. ('Justice should be blind and friendless.') As he grew older, Henry was 'said to be one of the finest boys of his age that Englishmen had ever clapped eyes on'. Ben Jonson even predicted a hero of a stature commensurate with that of the Black Prince. The King's advice on the waging of war was therefore appropriate: 'First let the justice of your cause be your greatest strength and then omit not to use all lawful means for the backing of the same ... Choose old experienced captains and young soldiers ... be severe in discipline ... Be slow in taking on a war and slow too in making peace; an honourable and just war is more tolerable an evil than a disadvantageous peace.'

Among 'indifferent things', the King gave guidance on food ('let all your foods be of simples without composition of sauces, which are more like medicine than meat'); clothes ('be also modest in your raiment, neither over superfluous, like a debauched waster; nor yet over base like a miserable peddler'); and mode of speech ('be not sparing in your courtesies').

James, a homosexual who preferred the company of handsome young men to that of women, nevertheless gave a balanced view of matrimony. Marriage was

'... one of the greatest occasions that a man doeth in all his time, especially in taking his first wife. Marry then a godlie and virtuous wife, for she must be nearer unto you than any other companion. Flesh of your flesh, bone of your bone (as God himself said to Adam), and because I know not but God may call me before ye be readie for marriage, I will shortlie set down to you here my advice thereon:

'First of all consider that marriage is the greatest earthly felicity or misery that can come to a man. Keep your body clean and unpolluted and so give it to your wife to whom onlie it belongeth ... Be not ashamed then to keep clean your bodie which is the Temple of the Holy Spirit notwithstanding all allourments to the contrarie, for how can ye justlie crave to be joined to a good and pure virgin if your body be polluted ... Why should one be clean and the other defiled?'

On this point he bade Henry to recall the fate of his great-grandfather, who had suffered the loss of two sons and had to leave his throne to a daughter as retribution for his transgression. In an age of religious strife, James also counselled his son not to marry outside his own religion:

'... strait advice and difficult since the number of princesses of power and account professing our religion be very small, yet disagreement in religion brings with it disagreement in manners ... neither prid ye that ye will be able to frame her and make her as ye please! That deceiveth Solomon, the wisest King that ever was! ... Choose you a wife as I advise you to choose your servants, that she be of a whole, clean race, not subjected to hereditary sickness of the soule or bodie; for if a man be careful to breed horses and dogs of good kinds, how much more careful should he be for the bread of his own loins?'

Finally James recommended to his son the study of history, the scriptures and the laws of the land. 'Study to know your own craft, which is to rule your people ...'

Lord Macaulay, the historian, described James as 'made up of two men – a witty, well-read scholar who wrote, disputed and harangued, and a nervous drivelling idiot who acted'. There is ample evidence to confirm James's love of dialectics and he sometimes felt it necessary that Henry should sit at his side listening to these 'disputes' on such topics as: Do saints and angels know the secrets of the heart? Would it be lawful to kill a stranger and enemy who had been detained in a hostile port by adverse winds contrary to what had been stipulated in a truce? Do children imbibe the temper with the milk of their nurses? One feels inclined to classify such subjects as mentally indigestible for one so young.

Henry was not yet twelve when he matriculated at Magdalen College, Oxford, where he was presented with a pair of Oxford gloves and dined 'sitting alone in the midst of the upper table with the noblemen and courtiers in the middle of the hall and the Fellows and students on both sides of it'. For some unaccountable reason, the King vetoed a move to admit Henry as Master of Arts. At sixteen the young Prince was created Prince of Wales and established in a household of his own. Its magnificence excited jealousy in James and when, in the following year, Henry sought a niche for himself as President of the Council – an appointment that, admittedly, would have meant sharing executive power with the King – his request was refused. But for his untimely death the Prince – as Henry IX – might have been in a constitutional sense one of England's most formidable kings.

Until Henry's demise his brother Charles, Duke of York, had lived a secluded existence, partly because he was 'weak in body' and could not speak until the age of four; at one period James had actually contemplated encasing his legs in iron and cutting his tongue. Another suggestion, however, has been submitted for the boy's seclusion. As there seemed to be no future for Charles in secular life, thoughts had turned to the Church, with the archbishopric of Canterbury being suggested. Maybe this early inclination to the Church of England moulded Charles's attitude years later, when he resolutely disagreed with its disestablishment. His refusal would cost him his life, for he died on the scaffold as much for his religious as for his political convictions.

Accidentally, or wisely, James, who spent more on jewels for his sons than on books, chose well when he engaged the kindly Thomas Murray for his son's 'paedagogue', paying him stipend in the form of authority to collect debts due to the attainted and deceased Duke of Somerset, Lord Hussey and Archbishop Cranmer. As with his brother, learning came naturally to Charles, as is abundantly clear from his early correspondence. His letters reflect his infectious charm, as, for instance: 'Sweet, sweet father, i learn to decline substantives and adjectives. Give me your blessing.' It is likely that many of the letters in Latin, though signed by Charles, were composed by his tutor, as a document from King James to Murray and now in the Bodleian Library suggests:

'Considering the pains and travails employed by you, not only in the careful education of our dearly beloved son the prince, and instructing him in all kinds of good learning, according to the capacity of his tender years, but also in penning and framing his missive letters in divers languages, directly to ourself or foreign princes, we are willing both to testify your acceptance of this your service, formerly done, and to encourage you with the like faithfulness and diligence to prosecute the same. Therefore, we have thought good to command you to continue the penning and writing of all such missives as shall be directly by our dearly beloved son the prince ... giving and granting unto you ... the custody and keeping of our said son's signet.'

Charles, whose next tutor was Peter Young (who had taught both his father and his brother), was a competent linguist, although, most probably thanks to an embarrassing stammer, he could express himself better on paper. He was drawn to music and the fine arts and, being 'addicted to grave studies', was steeped in theology. The King would proudly boast to eminent churchmen: 'Charles can manage a point in theological controversy with the best-studied divine of you all.' Throughout his life Charles would be charmingly courteous but rather aloof. Bad health – the trauma of childhood – and Henry's brilliance and magnificent physique (which had seemed to exaggerate his own imperfections) had stamped introversion – the hallmark of his character – on the sensitive Charles. He hid an inferiority complex behind a false façade of calm. Briefly, Charles was un-approachable, and of the relatively few people whom he accepted in friendship, the most prominent was a man whose influence would be calamitous.

George Villiers, the future Duke of Buckingham, was the latest to ingratiate himself into the King's affections. As the power of the handsome 'Steenie', as he was known, over the King increased, so it did also over the heir apparent. It was an influence from which Charles should have been spared. History now knows its unfor-tunate aspects: the only good that emerged was the love of art that Villiers engendered in the Prince, for on his accession Charles amassed the most valuable collection of Renaissance paintings ever assembled in England. Some would be sold abroad – never to return – during Cromwell's rule, but others would survive to remain the nucleus of the finest royal collection in Europe – today known as the Queen's Collection.

During his formative years Charles witnessed a ceremony that would one day produce a chain of events that would terminate in a political time-bomb. It took place when he was an impressionable youth of thirteen. Scarcely were the tears dry for Prince Henry than his sister, Princess Elizabeth, was betrothed to the Elector Palatine, the Palsgrave Frederick. Mourning was still worn and although no one was aware of it then, from the union would be born the House of Hanover a century later (and later still the House of Windsor). In a sense that wedding was the funeral rite of the House of Stuart, for it would spell the end of that dynasty.

The maggot gnawing at the vitals of the Stuarts would be Parlia-ment. On Charles I's accession it would creep into the education of the son who, after the ordeal of war and exile, would inherit the throne as Charles II. An elaborate education had been devised for the 'unthankful', self-willed child, who developed an attachment for a block of wood, without which he refused to sleep at night. The Earl of Newcastle, the first to supervise the Prince of Wales's upbringing, detailed instructions in a letter to the Prince:

'It is fit you should have some languages, though I confess I would rather have you study things than words ... I would not have you too studious, for too much contemplation spoils action, and virtue consists in that.

'Study history so that you may compare the dead with the living, for the same humours is now as was then; there is no alteration but in names.'

There was still Divine Right to reckon with and Charles looked upon himself as God's deputy. He was advised to show devotion at prayers (thus setting an example to his people) and to be courteous to all. ('The putting off of your hat and making a leg please more than reward.')

Newcastle was wiser than some governors charged with the superintendence of other heirs apparent; he appreciated that anyone with Charles's temperament learns more from contact with life than from books. 'I would not have you too studious,' he had told the Prince. There were no fears on that account; circumstances would determine this. The thunder of the Civil War would soon reverberate across England. Charles was in his thirteenth year as he watched the opening battle at Edgehill with his brother James. With them was a tutor, Dr William Harvey, eminent as the discoverer of the circulation of blood. Harvey was more engrossed in a book than in observing war until a cannon-ball crashed through a hedge, making the trio scurry to safety. Charles would learn more about kingship and statesmanship through the hazards and anxieties of war and adversity in exile. It is ironical that one of the worst-educated heirs apparent due to the upheaval of war turned into one of the most subtle and shrewdest of monarchs at a critical time of religious and social conflict. This was the outcome of hard lessons learnt in crises.

At one point Parliament had interfered, claiming the right to collaborate in the Prince's training. Their choice of governor was John Hampden, a name that could do nothing other than incense the King. To Charles I this abrasive politician was the architect of most of his political ills and the firebrand of parliamentary malcontents. He not unnaturally objected to the Commons' choice.

While Charles was in exile the renowned Thomas Hobbes of Malmesbury taught him mathematics. Hobbes was in the forefront of scientific and philosophical thought and inspired the Prince's love of scientific discovery years later. As King he would encourage the founders of the Royal Society and conduct his own research in a laboratory at Whitehall Palace. But it was Newcastle who exercised the greatest influence in moulding Charles for kingship, advocating – as being preferable to book learning – the winning of 'people's hearts, and then you have all they have; more you cannot have'. The blueprint for kingship that this polished courtier and man of the world prepared was so much in accord with the Prince's temperament – a factor that was lamentably absent in the education devised for the Hanoverians. Indeed the Hanoverian dynasty gave a classic demonstration of how not to prepare an heir apparent for his kingly destiny.

On Sunday morning, 1 August 1714, after recurring bouts of sickness and recovery, the gouty Queen Anne – last of the Stuart monarchs – died in Kensington Palace. The raucous cries of 'No Hanover' were loud in the streets of London, but noisier still was the clamour of 'No popery'. By the terms of the Act of Settlement, George Louis, Elector of Hanover, was declared 'the lawful and rightful King of Great Britain, France and Ireland' and His Majesty was herewith 'to employ his utmost care in putting this kingdom into a happy and flourishing condition'. But George I, a 'proper-middle-siz'd well proportioned man ... not addicted to any diversions besides hunting', took his time. 'All the King-killers are on my side,' he said and already 'in the pockets of the Whigs'. Some weeks elapsed before he arrived in London with his son, George Augustus. Fog had delayed them and when they landed at Greenwich it was 18 September. It was the birth of the Hanoverian dynasty in Britain, a period of metamorphosis in the constitutional sense. One might have expected the xenophobic British to rebel, for a while at least, against the German newcomers, but apart from Jacobite undercurrents the Hanoverians were received with tolerance.

There was no reason why the heir apparent should not be educated in the traditional manner, then serve on the Council and as regent in the King's absence. To the astonishment of the British, this pattern was not followed. For a reason as yet never adequately explained, the early Hanoverian sovereigns possessed an inordinate hatred for their first-born children. Hence from the outset father and son entertained a profound loathing for one another. Some say that the enmity was congenital, but maybe the first George detested his heir simply because he was a constant memento of his wife, Sophia Dorothea of Zell. In Hanover George had neglected and ill-treated her, accusing her of misconduct with the Swedish Count Königsmarck, an accusation that she strenuously denied. The stolid George brushed aside her pleas. After he had divorced her in 1694

Sophia languished as a prisoner in the castle at Ahlden until her death thirty-two years later.

George I's notorious infidelities and harsh treatment of his wife may account for the son's contempt for his hypocritical father. The King had brought to London two Protestant paramours – the stout Frau von Kilmansegge and the scraggy Fräulein von Schulenberg – royal whores who, ennobled by the King, were quickly satirized as 'The Elephant' and 'The Maypole'. On ministerial advice the King readily created his son the Prince of Wales, not out of paternal regard but because this grasping monarch thought he could thereby tap a new source of wealth. Regrettably for the Prince, the dignity did not enhance his status. When the King left for his beloved Hanover he refused to appoint his heir as regent. Only fear of public reaction compelled him to compromise; the Prince was appointed 'Guardian of the Realm and Lieutenant within the Same', a title redolent of the days of the Black Prince.

So far the Prince's apprenticeship for kingship had been nil. Now, with his father out of the country, he 'took a turn of being civil to everybody and applied himself to be well with the King's ministers and to understand the state of the nation', as Sir Robert Walpole explained. To acquire knowledge of his future duties was laudable, but the ministers, conscious of family friction, doubted his motives. Did he merely wish to anger the King? They knew that George would be resentful if the news reached him, yet they dare not offend their future sovereign. The King himself resolved their dilemma: information leaked to Hanover and he immediately returned to denigrate his son. In the meantime, however, the Prince of Wales had won enormous popularity among the people. This was his strongest weapon, for in a constitutional sense there was no other means of support.

The smouldering royal conflict burst into flames at the christening of the Prince's son, an event that was held in the Princess of Wales's bedroom at St James's Palace. It was a unique occasion: not for almost four centuries – since the Black Prince – had a Prince of Wales had issue during his father's life. George Augustus had requested his father and his uncle, the Bishop of Osnabrück, to be his infant's godfathers, and the King had acquiesced. But he arrived with the Duke of Newcastle, the Lord Chamberlain, as co-sponsor – a move calculated to annoy the Prince. It was common knowledge that George Augustus detested the Duke, but to replace a royal godparent with a commoner was gross humiliation. The choleric Prince could contain his emotions no longer. 'Rascal, I will find you out,' he shouted, shaking his fist at the Duke. A duel seemed inevitable and the King, furious at the Prince's outburst, ordered him to be arrested and confined to his room. Horrified ministers induced the King to remove the guard, but when Caroline, Princess of Wales, was fully recovered she and her husband were given notice to quit and to leave their children behind. The scandal was the talk of London and street hawkers reaped profits from a ballad called 'The Christening'. Ironically the life of the infant Duke of Gloucester was short and the Duke of Newcastle had to supervise his godson's funeral.

The public sympathy stimulated by the separation of the Prince and Princess from their children led to their custody being contested in January 1718 before twelve learned judges at Serjeant's Inn. One thousand years of history were probed to find precedents, but in vain. The court was asked to consider whether 'the education and care of the persons of His Majesty's grandchildren, the ordering of their place of abode, the appointment of their governors ... attendants and servants and the care and protection of their interests when grown up, belonged as of right to His Majesty the King of this realm, or to the Prince of Wales'. Perhaps to avoid the King's wrath, a majority of ten, including the Lord Chief Justice, decided that as the King held right of marriage over his grandchildren, then the same applied to their education, since this was of greater significance than marriage. The Lord Chancellor, one of the dissenting minority of two, lost his chancellorship; an earldom was conferred on the Lord Chief Justice.

Several years elapsed before Walpole diplomatically arranged at least the façade of a reconciliation. The family quarrel had endangered the throne; the Jacobites, Walpole told the King, might profit from domestic strife. George received his son after the latter had submitted a formal apology. The meeting was brief; the King, almost incoherent, could only exclaim in French : 'But your conduct! Your conduct!' An official announcement described the reconciliation the next day. However, if a contemporary account is accurate, the atmosphere was less than cordial – 'the King's court was still at the top of the room, and the Prince's hung about at the bottom behind him ... The Prince looked down and behaved prodegious well and the King cast an angry look that way every now and then. One could not help thinking it was like a Dog and Cat, whenever the dog stirs a foot the cat sets up her back and is ready to fly at him ... Such a crowd as was never seen, for not only curiosity but interest had brought them together.'

In June 1727, on his fifth visit to Hanover, George I died without warning. Receiving the news at midday three days later, Walpole hastened to Richmond, to the country house of George Augustus. The Prince, his afternoon rest disturbed, came towards Walpole, his breeches in his hand. 'Dat is one big lie,' he is alleged to have told Walpole on learning of his father's death. But it was true; he was proclaimed George II the next day.

While rummaging among the late King's papers, Queen Caroline discovered in his cabinet a document written by Charles Stanhope. To her astonishment she came across a proposal from Admiral Lord Berkeley to kidnap the Prince of Wales and transport him to America – 'where he would never be heard of more'. (It is interesting to recall that the name of Berkeley had occurred in another tragedy. Centuries earlier the first Prince of Wales, as Edward II, had been foully murdered at Berkeley Castle.) The King had not acted on the proffered advice, but it seems that he had pondered on it. This, and his attempt to disinherit his son from the electorate of Hanover – a plot that foundered due to ministerial non-compliance – mirrored the father's burning animosity towards his heir.

This curious sadistic streak would be repeated down the Hano-verian line, a distasteful characteristic that sets it apart from royal dynasties in England. It would carry on right down to Queen Victoria and end happily in the reign of Edward VII. As yet no one has supplied an acceptable explanation. Paternal jealousy and fear of a popular heir menacing the throne hardly represent a basic cause, although rival courts and the manipulation of the prince by un-scrupulous politicians exacerbated relationships. In this strained relationship, the sovereign impeded the training of the heir apparent. In previous dynasties it had been accepted that the heir should be groomed to understudy the sovereign and some princes had depu-tized for their fathers even in adolescence; the Black Prince, for example, had been named Guardian of England when only eight. True, the real onus of decision-making rested with the ministers; but from it all the royal apprentice – like Prince Charles today – slowly learnt the intricacies of the Council and Parliament and equipped himself with the knowledge and experience needed for kingship. The heir of Henry IV was dismissed as Council President, but this exception was inspired by the usurper's uneasy conscience. Unfortunately Queen Victoria would quote this incident when she herself was approached for employment by her son.

It is odd that, although great constitutional (and indeed social and industrial) changes occurred under the Hanoverians, the training and employment of the heirs apparent were abysmal. Typical was the attitude of George II towards his heir, Frederick Louis of Hanover. Left in Hanover by George in the care of governors and tutors, apparently to convince the people that they still retained their electoral prince, Frederick – a 'florid, milk-faced kind of boy' – waited fourteen years before following his parents to England. And his arrival was solely due to public murmuring: people resented the fact that the heir apparent was utterly devoid of English training. Finally the King did budge, but only when faced with the threat of an address from Parliament.

The young Prince arrived in London one winter's night with no one to greet him, later receiving a cool embrace from Queen Caroline, his mother, and two fingers of his father's hand – hardly an emotional reunion. 'Yesterday,' announced the *Daily Post* on 8 December 1728, 'His Royal Highness, Prince Frederick, came to Whitechapel about seven in the evening and proceeded thence privately in a hackney coach to St James's. His Royal Highness alighted at the Friary, and walked down to the Queen's backstairs, and was thence conducted to Her Majesty's apartment.' The Queen's maternal instincts were no less lukewarm than the King's attitude. Once she was heard to remark: 'My dear first-born is the greatest ass and the greatest liar and the greatest *canaille* and the greatest beast in the whole world, and I heartily wish he were out of it.' As far as their temperaments allowed, George II and Queen Caroline bestowed affection on their other children, but the King's conduct towards his heir was even worse than his own treatment by his father. For a reason never accounted for, George II despised Frederick Louis even in infancy, and in later life would ignore him when they were in the same room. Frederick, a contemporary observed, was a ghost visible to everyone except his father. Gossips indulged in an orgy of speculation, one innuendo arising from Frederick's dark complexion. Irresponsible tongues drew attention to Mustapha and Mahomet, his grandfather's Turkish servants, to whom, they said, he bore a striking resemblance. Although these wild, scandalous insinuations lack foundation, the mystery of the hatred of both parents for their first-born has yet to be solved. They even tried to deny him his lawful succession to the throne. Either ignorant or contemptuous of the British constitution, as Prince and Princess of Wales they intended, on the death of George 1, to disinherit him, allowing William, their second son, to succeed to the throne. Both George 1 and Walpole scotched this nefarious plan. Whether or not he knew of the proposal, Frederick, who was deliberately kept short of money, later offered to relinquish his claim to Hanover in Prince William's favour if he could receive the annual £100,000 to which he was entitled. With customary malignance, the Queen angrily defiled her son as 'an avaricious, sordid monster, so little able to resist taking a guinea on any terms that if the Pretender were to offer him £500,000 for the reversion of the Crown he would say : "Give me the money" '.

'Poor Fred' was created Prince of Wales, but death deprived him of the throne; he died from a burst abscess caused by a blow from a cricket ball while playing with his children. When Lord Bute conveyed the sad news, the King went across to his mistress and remarked : *'Fritz ist todt'*, then resumed his place at the card-table.

Prince Frederick Louis illustrates that the harm or good done by a sovereign depends on the education he receives as heir apparent and on parental will. By training and temperament, the first two Georges were essentially German in outlook and ways; both reached their new country too late to be moulded into Englishmen. But other things apart, neither of them ever concealed their preference for Hanover, disliking Britain and all things British. Frederick Louis was cast in the same Teutonic mould, but he had the wisdom to realize that for the good of both Britain and the dynasty, a future King of England must be trained on British lines.

This was in his mind when he planned the upbringing of George William Frederick, his eldest son. His 'political will' contained 'Instructions for my Son George, drawn up my-Self for His Good, that of my Family and for that of His People, according to the ideas of my Grandfather, and best friend, George 1'. Not wishing to leave his son 'a Sermon as is usually done by Persons of My Rank', he commended him to be 'Just, Humane, Generous and Brave, to live with economy and try not to spend more in the year than the Malt and two shillings in the Land Tax'. He further advised him to separate Hanover from England, to avoid wars and to 'convince the Nation that You are not only an Englishman born and bred, but you are also this by inclination'. He bestowed paternal benevolence on his family and was himself adored by his eldest son, and it is reasonable to assume that if he had ascended the throne, the shocking pattern of antagonism between father and heir would have been halted. Whether any other benefits would have accrued in the reign of Frederick I is open to doubt.

Unfortunately the tuition of his eldest son was mismanaged from the outset: governors and tutors came and went according to the whims of political fortune. The boy's first tutor was Dr Francis Ayscough, whose qualifications rested with his skill in managing Prince Frederick's privy purse. Often he was more indolent than his royal pupil. By the age of eleven George had learnt some Latin, but to the dismay of Augusta, the Princess of Wales, he had made scant progress in English. To appease her anxieties, George Scott was engaged as an extra teacher. To his consternation, his efforts more or less failed to inspire the princely mind. Once George attributed his failure to fulfil some exercise as 'constitutional idleness'. 'Idleness?' protested Scott. 'Yours is not idleness. Your brother Edward is idle, but you must not call being asleep all day being idle.'

To his ultimate disadvantage, the future George III (who, incidentally, intrigues Prince Charles more than any other monarch in British history) also suffered from a surfeit of maternal devotion. In what appears to have been a chronic state of anguish because of his indolence and immaturity, his mother declared that his education gave her 'much pain; his book-learning she was no judge of, though she supposed it small and useless'. He was not a dissipated boy, she protested, 'but good-natured and cheerful with a serious cast of mind, and those about him know him no more than if they had never seen him'.

Whatever Prince George's deficiencies, his earlier tutors scarcely created the ideal environment in which a backward child might thrive. Four of them fell to quarrelling among themselves, and one was falsely accused of imprinting Jacobitism on his pupil's mind.

By now the education of the heir apparent had become a matter of public concern. Pamphlets were distributed conveying criticism and displeasure and the King, ousting George's governor, Lord Harcourt, replaced him with a reluctant Lord Waldegrave. Yet in the end he would report that though George had received tuition from 'men of learning, and worthy, good men, they had but little weight and influence. The mother and the nursery always prevailed.' When Frederick died, the widowed Princess doubtless dominated her son's mind, even to the point of rebelling at times against his paternal grandfather. On one occasion the ageing monarch, abandoning his kingly dignity, lost control of himself and struck his grandson. In days to come, George would tell his children of the incident. Years later his son, the Duke of Sussex, accompanying a friend of J. Heneage Jesse, the biographer of George II, to Hampton Court, exclaimed: 'I wonder in which of these rooms it was that George II struck my father. The blow so disgusted him with the place that he could never afterwards be induced to think of it as a residence.'

Queen Augusta resolutely resisted political pressure, commanding her son 'to be a King' and impregnating his mind with the political beliefs of Henry St John, Viscount Bolingbroke, author of *The Patriot King*. They would form his political creed when he reached the throne. Bolingbroke visualized a supreme monarch, remote above all elements of society, and invested with the right to decide on issues according to his absolute power. It was a return to absolutism, to the monarchical rights that the first two Georges – looking upon Britain as a means of enriching themselves – had accidentally or indifferently abandoned to Parliament. As was to be expected, the governing class, the greater landed aristocracy, viewed this new conception of monarchy rather sourly.

Happily for Augusta, John Stuart, the third Earl of Bute, now rallied to her cause. This genial Scot, who apparently manifested great pride in his shapely legs, endorsed Bolingbroke's philosophical outpourings. But another factor may have entered into his close alliance with the Princess of Wales. All the evidence implies that Augusta was entranced by the Scottish laird, an attitude that her husband does not seem to have shared. Not long before his death he had referred to Bute as 'only fit to be an ambassador in some paltry little court where there is nothing to do'. Augusta, however, must have noticed other qualities, for Horace Walpole was 'as convinced of their amorous relation as if he had seen them together', and Lord Waldegrave, who, as George's governor, must have witnessed much in the Wales's household, considered that Augusta had found in the Scotsman 'accomplishments of which the Prince her husband may not perhaps have been the most competent judge'.

For Bute the association would reap rich dividends: on the death of the King the young George III elevated his mentor to the rank of

Chief Minister – an honour in the United Kingdom never previously accorded to a Scot. For years he would impose his overbearing self on George, both as Prince of Wales and sovereign. Long afterwards Junius, crystallizing this unfortunate relationship in his famous letter, would say :

'The plan of tutelage and future dominion over the heir apparent laid many years ago at Carlton House, between the Princess Dowager and her favourite, the Earl of Bute, was as gross and palpable as that which was concerted between Anne of Austria and Cardinal Mazarin to govern Lewis the Fourteenth, and in effect to prolong his minority until the end of their lives. That Prince had strong natural parts and used frequently to blush for his own ignorance and want of education which had been wilfully neglected by his mother and her minion ... When it was proposed to settle the present King's household as Prince of Wales, it is well known that the Earl of Bute was forced into it in direct contradiction to the late King's inclination. That was the salient point from which all the mischiefs and disgraces of the present reign took life and motion. From that moment Lord Bute never suffered the Prince of Wales to be an instant out of his sight. We need look no further.'

That was the unpardonable action of Augusta as well as of Bute. Whether it was actuated by selfish or merely misguided motives, she foolishly withheld from him the society of people of his own age, other than his brothers and sisters. Her sincere aim was to train her son for kingship, but her tactics did irreparable harm. Ridiculously – though her intentions may have been praiseworthy – she shuddered at the thought of his being polluted by contact with the outside world. When she was told that it was 'much to be wished that the Prince conversed more with the people who have some knowledge of the world', the Princess remonstrated : 'The young people of the day are ill-educated and so vicious that they frighten me.'

If the warm-hearted Frederick had lived perhaps much would have been different. As it was, Prince George was deplorably ignorant of men and affairs, a deficiency that marred his reign. The King of Hanover, his son, would write in 1845 : 'To tell you the honest truth, the impression on my mind has ever been that it was a very unfortunate circumstance for my father that he was kept, as it were aloof ... from all young men of his own age; and this I saw evident marks of almost daily.'

As a memorandum in his own handwriting shows, Frederick was interested in his children's education. Writing to Lord North, their

first governor, on 14 October 1750, he instructed him that George
and Edward, his brother, should rise at seven in the morning. From
eight until nine they were to read with Mr Scott — 'and he to stay
with 'em till the Doctor come [Dr John Thomas]', who would teach
from nine to eleven, after which a Mr Fung was in charge for an
hour. From noon until 12.30 someone of the name of Rupert was
in attendance — 'but Mr Fung to remain there'. Then the Princes
were 'to Their Play hour till 3 o'clock'. Dinner was served at three
o'clock and three times a week, 'at half an hour past four, Desnoyer
comes. At 5, Mr Fung till half an hour past 6. At half an hour past 6
till 8 Mr Scot. At 8 supper. Between 9 and 10, in Bed. On Sunday,
Prayers exactly at half an hour past 9 o'clock. Then the two eldest
Princes, and the two eldest Princesses, are to go to Prince George's
apartment, to be instructed by Dr Ayscough in the Principles of
Religion till 11 o'clock.'

When George was installed as a Knight of the Garter, Frederick
now and again organized extra-curricular subjects for his eldest son.
Why he considered them necessary is not known, but a popular
lampoon informs us of these nocturnal rovings:

> Now Frederick's a knight and George is a knight,
> With stalls in Windsor Chapel,
> We'll hope they'll prowl no more by night,
> To look at garters black and white
> Or legs of female rabble.

But the father discovered that the son was no less bored with
feminine charm than with daytime studies. To that extent George
was a misfit among the Hanoverians, among whom debauchery and
moral laxity were accepted. Thanks to his tutors, or to his own
natural inclinations, the young Prince, unlike his sophisticated
brother, was both pious and morally pure. Not long after the death
of their father the two Princes were playing near their mother when
Edward suddenly remarked: 'Brother, when you and I are grown,
you shall be married but I will keep a mistress.' 'Be quiet, Eddy,'
scolded George, 'we shall have anger presently for your nonsense.
There must be no mistresses at all.' At that moment Augusta broke
in: 'What you say? You had more need learn your pronouns, as
the preceptor bid you do. Can you tell what is a pronoun?' 'Yes,'
replied the young Duke. 'A pronoun is to a noun what a mistress is
to a wife, a substitute and a representative.'

As Lord Waldegrave revealed, George was 'strictly honest', and we can accept his truthfulness. But the manner in which he tried to fashion his children's characters and minds was questionable. Since he had suffered in his own education through political influences, it would have been rational for him to safeguard his eldest son (who was created Prince of Wales when only five days old) from a similar fate. Yet as George III he condoned the practice, provided the tutors belonged to the faction he favoured. There were times, too, when he appointed teachers according to his own whims. Once, having done so, he was asked by the Duke of Leeds if he had sought the advice of anyone. In high dudgeon the King answered sharply : 'Surely I am master to appoint whom I like for the education of my children.'

A corps of tutors, with Lord Holderness in charge, undertook to train the Prince from the age of nine. Foremost was Dr William Markham, Bishop of Chester, who would become Archbishop of York. He had been headmaster of Westminster School – at that time the leading nursery of prime ministers and other statesmen. Markham and his colleagues were instructed to apply the severest discipline and flog the Prince whenever a flogging was merited.

Discipline was indeed extremely strict. In later life the Duke of Sussex would recall the time when, breathing heavily from asthma, he was told to stop making a noise. Unable to do so, he was thrashed for disobedience. Times had certainly changed. Centuries earlier it would have been outrageous to inflict pain on the heir apparent's sacred person; someone else would have received punishment on his behalf.

Dr Dodd set Prince George exemplary exercises in penmanship but would later be hanged for forgery. Walpole submitted his ideas on what should be the basis of the Prince's training : there should be two salient points : 'The first that he should not be trusted to anything but a ductile cypher; the other that he should be brought up with due affection for regal power; in other words, he was to be the slave of his father and the tyrant of the people.'

The curriculum catered for seven hours' study daily, offering the typical education of an eighteenth-century gentleman. But whether it befitted a future constitutional monarch is debatable. An innovation was a simplified form of 'husbandry'. The Prince was instructed on how to grow his own plot of wheat, how to thresh the wheat and, when the grain had been milled, how to bake bread. The King – nicknamed 'Farmer' George – fostered agricultural development and founded model farms at Windsor, and wanted his son to acquaint

himself with the people's central occupation; but just as the King
was fascinated by machinery and physical science – and in some
ways ahead of his time – so the Prince leaned towards the artistic
sphere. In years to come his influence would be apparent, particularly in architecture, and he would add many old masters to the
royal collections. His temperament was not attuned to the correcti-
tude of his father's court, which, in the words of Edmund Burke, had
'lost all that was stately and venerable in the antique manners, without retrenching anything of the cumbrous charge of a Gothic
establishment'.

Palace life for the children was as dull as the food. A contemporary London newspaper commented: 'The Royal children by His
Majesty's command get up early, have bread and milk for breakfast
and dine on broth and salads, seldom being allowed any butcher's
meat, their solids being chiefly chicken. They drink no liquor other
than whey and milk and water and are sometimes indulged with a
glass of weak negus [hot sweetened wine and water]. Supper is the
same as breakfast.'

The Prince's later reaction to his father was not surprising.
Talented when he wished to apply himself, he resented the fact that
his natural instincts were suppressed. What was also irksome as he
grew older was his realization of his high status and of the fact
that he had been stripped of its privileges. Invitations to country
houses went unaccepted because the King forbade him to go. Indeed
his father denied him the companionship not merely of more
ordinary folk but also of the nobility. He still wore a child's frilled
collar when he was sixteen years old. Not unexpectedly, he was
provoked into angry outbursts towards both his tutors and the King.
It is on record that he banged on the door of the King's bedroom,
shouting the cries of a nearby mob, as they chanted: 'Wilkes for
ever! No. 45 for ever.'

One tutor, Richard Hurd, Bishop of Worcester, predicted that the
Prince of Wales, then fifteen, would become 'either the most polished
gentleman or the most accomplished blackguard in Europe – perhaps
an admixture of both'. This 'stupid, odious German, sergeant-major
system of discipline' began to evoke open criticism. As one critic
has written: 'The education of the Prince of Wales was conducted
on a plan perfectly well calculated to render him a respectable
scholar and an accomplished gentleman; but, on the other hand, it

Prince Charles (born 14 November 1948), a few weeks old with his mother, then Princess Elizabeth. (*Cecil Beaton*)

Charles learning the rudiments of the art of the camera. (*Radio Times Hulton Picture Library*)

Cheam School, whose roots stretch back to the reign of Charles I; it has a long-standing connection with the Mountbatten family, to which the Duke of Edinburgh belongs. (*Keystone Press Agency*)

Old boy and new pupil. Prince Philip and Prince Charles greeted by the headmaster on the latter's first day at Gordonstoun. (*London Express*)

Pestered by press photographers, the young Prince takes his first lessons in ski-ing at Tarasp, Switzerland. (*Camera Press*)

Mixing with many admirers at Sydney. (*Keystone Press Agency*)

Pre-history (physical and social), anthropology and archaeology were the royal undergraduate's personal choice of subjects for study. (*Camera Press*)

Sharing jokes with two members of the former Goon team — Harry Secombe (left) and Spike Milligan — at the Eccentric Club, London. (*Keystone Press Agency*)

Sometimes Prince Charles made his own meals in the kitchen installed by Sandringham workmen. (*Keystone Press Agency — C.P.N.A.*)

Taking part in a sketch in one of the Trinity College revues. (*Keystone Press Agency*)

Prince Charles's first interview for television — a prelude to the Caernarvon ceremony. (*Camera Press*)

The Prince of Wales at Buckingham Palace wearing the ceremonial uniform of the Royal Regiment of Wales. (*Camera Press*)

In the ancient Order of the Garter, the Prince of Wales is second in status after the Queen. (*Keystone Press Agency*)

Prince Charles with the veteran yachtsman Uffa Fox sailing off the Isle of Wight. (*Camera Press*)

As Duke of Cornwall, Prince Charles meets some of his tenants at Daglingworth. (*Camera Press*)

Prince Charles is noted for his witty after-dinner speeches. Here he is addressing The Pilgrims, a society promoting Anglo-American understanding. (*Keystone Press Agency*)

Meeting the people. In a series of visits to industrial and government establishments, Prince Charles went to the Bankside Power Station, London. (*Keystone Press Agency*)

Left: Prince Charles competing with Prince Philip for the ball in a polo match. (*Associated Newspapers*)

Below: At Longchamp races, Prince Charles in conversation with Madame Michel Cointat, wife of the French Minister of Agriculture. (*Camera Press*)

Prince Charles, a naval pilot, at the controls of a Wessex 5 commando helicopter. (*Camera Press*)

Opposite above: In Kenya for a two-week visit, Prince Charles is greeted by a Turkana elder. (*Keystone Press Agency*)

Opposite below: Sharing a joke while on a safari in Kenya. (*Camera Press*)

A monarch in the making. Prince Charles feels that there is much he can do if he is 'given the chance to do it'. (*Camera Press*)

was ill calculated to make him either a prudent prince or a great monarch.'

George III was inconsistent. In the heir apparent's infancy he had been eager to exhibit his son to public view. For instance, before he was three years old he had addressed his first deputation. When seven, ornate in scarlet and gold and wearing the insignia of the Garter, he and the Princess Royal had held their first Drawing Room. Yet as the Prince grew towards manhood the King withheld him from the outer world. Not until he was almost of age was he permitted to appear at a ball, and then simply to appease the Spanish ambassador. It is possible, then, that the defects in the Prince's character that came to the fore in adult life were born in childhood and adolescence. Even if these shortcomings were innate, it is fair to say that they were nurtured by a system that was too austere. One weakness was his unreadiness to speak the truth. 'A lie is ever ready when it is wanted,' accused the King.

If the Prince can be believed, this deplorable trait was instilled in himself and his brothers and sisters by their mother. 'The Queen taught us to equivocate,' he said. At least he had the courage to admit his faults and he tried to protect his daughter, Princess Charlotte, from that failing. Preparing her education, he felt morally bound to write : 'Above all, I must teach her to speak the truth. You know that I do not speak the truth and that my brothers don't.'

The man who became George IV has been hailed as the most scandalous Prince of Wales since Henry V (assuming that Henry's antics were fact and not fiction) and the most cultivated since Charles I. But perhaps the key to it all was the King's adamant refusal to give him employment. Even a commission in the army or a visit to his future subjects was refused. The King, who rose at 5 a.m., scolded the Prince for rising late. 'I find, Sir,' came the frank reply, 'however late I rise, that the day is long enough for doing nothing.' Thus emerged a complex personality, whom Sir Llewellyn Woodward has summarized as 'a clever, versatile, lazy man, of some taste in architecture and painting, attractive and rude by turns, but always a liar ... He was a fair judge of character, but he never used his judgment for the good of the state, and never concerned himself with anything which did not ... affect his own pleasure.'

Of the last three Princes of Wales, reference has been made elsewhere. In the case of the future Edward VII, Queen Victoria and

Prince Albert laboured heroically to equip their eldest son for kingship. Whereas at the worst ordinary boys endure school reports twice or three times yearly, Prince Albert Edward suffered the ordeal each day. With the possible exception of one tutor, the Reverend Henry Birch, who understood the lonely boy (but was dismissed when a genuine friendship arose between tutor and pupil), no attempt was made to study the character of the young Prince. All the cramming could not alter the fact that Albert Edward was not academically inclined. His talents were for social life through which he rendered skilful service in diplomacy.

His second son was never intended to be King George v and would have devoted his life to the Royal Navy but for the death of his elder brother. He knew scarcely anything outside the world of the professional sailor, but luckily he possessed qualities that were ideal in the difficult circumstances of his reign. Thus he is remembered as a good and patriotic king. He considered that his own system of education – private tutors followed by naval training at Osborne and Dartmouth – was so ideal for kingship that he chose it for his heir, who reigned briefly as Edward viii. Whether the latter's failure as a monarch can be attributed to defects in his character or in his upbringing is arguable. But the errors made by Queen Victoria and Prince Albert in the education of his grandfather echoed in his own childhood and youth. Between himself and his great-nephew Prince Charles there is also a parallel: from the time of birth neither could escape from being a child of destiny; each was marked out as a future king.

8 An Important Birthday

But for Protestantism and a bloodless revolution, Prince Charles would never have stood within the shadow of the throne. In the seventeenth century – in the dramatic clash between the monarchy and Parliament – a predominantly Protestant England tolerated its Catholic sovereign James II solely in the belief that there was no papist progeny to succeed him, since his Protestant first wife, Anne Hyde, had given him two daughters. But in the summer of 1687 the King and his second wife, Mary of Modena, prayed together at a shrine in Wales. This act of piety attracted little attention until some months later, when the nation was besought to pray that the Queen might become 'a joyful mother of children ... and the King live to see his children's children around his throne'.

The non-Catholics were appalled, unable to face with equanimity the prospect of a papist prince succeeding an increasingly tyrannical papist father. Fears mingled with ribaldry, and Lord Clarendon was impelled to write: 'It is strange to see how the Queen's being with child is everywhere ridiculed as if scarcely anybody believed it to be true.' But the scoffing soon ceased. James Francis Edward, 'well formed and of full size,' was born on 10 June 1688 – Trinity Sunday. Oxford celebrated the event in verse, recalling that another Edward, the illustrious Black Prince, had also entered this world on Trinity Sunday, some three and a half centuries earlier. The Lord Mayor and Corporation of London presented the infant with a purse of gold; in Rome the Papacy rejoiced at the thought of Catholic continuity and, as if to consolidate the future, the Pope agreed to be the infant's godfather.

In England there was more anger than joy. The Protestant Whigs even cast doubts on the child's legitimacy. The basis for this calumny was spurious: it concerned a document that was placed in the baby's hand when he was five weeks old, petitioning for an increase in the number of London's hackney cabs to swell the revenue from

taxes for the feeding and upbringing of foundling children. Deliberately or unwittingly, the King's opponents 'found significance in
this precocious solicitude for illegitimates'. Other factors, they
argued, implied a sinister plot. Queen Mary had been borne to St
James's Palace at night, choosing a room with a door near the bed-
head. The non-Catholics vehemently spread the unfounded rumour
that the child was not the King's son but a foundling smuggled into
the Queen's bedchamber in a warming-pan. Rumour vied with
rumour when the Prince developed 'the grippes'. In desperation the
Queen engaged the young wife of a tilemaker for the royal nursery,
where the ailing child took 'the suck' and began to revive. Indeed his
recovery was so speedy that hearsay now claimed that a healthy
child had been substituted for one that was dead.

Despite his rejoicing, James could not discount the swelling cry
of 'No popery!'. Intrigue was rife and rebellion was astir when a
powerful cabal, symbolizing most of the nation's great families, invited William of Orange, who had married Mary, the King's Protestant daughter, to 'bring over an army and secure the infringed
liberties' of England. While William waited for a favourable wind
to invade, James decided to act. Addressing an Extraordinary Council, he accused his enemies of maliciously corrupting the minds of
the people so that many now doubted whether 'the son with which
God hath blessed me is but a supposed child'. Fortunately this falsehood could be destroyed, for 'by particular Providence scarce any
prince was ever born where so many people were present'. Sixty-
seven people had witnessed the birth and the King now called more
than forty of them to offer testimony. Having assured, or so he believed, his son's succession, James now tried to cope with 'Dutch
Billy', who landed at Torbay a fortnight later. But the odds were too
weighted. London seethed with discontent and when he tried to dispatch his son to France, he was foiled by a law of the land: the heir
to the throne could not quit the country unless Parliament allowed
it. The child's guardians, who were stopped at Portsmouth, returned
safely to London, but two Catholic regiments sent to protect them
were scattered by the mob. In the turmoil the King arranged for the
Queen and the child, who had already been created Prince of Wales,
to be smuggled from England, promising to follow his distressed
consort within twenty-four hours.

Stealing from the Palace in disguise, the Queen crossed the Thames
by ferry, lurked for a while beneath a wall in Lambeth, then was

taken with her son to Gravesend, where a ship was waiting. The news was soon circulated that the 'Queen went down the river yesterday morning (10 December 1688) with the Prince of Wales and it is believed that she has gone to France. The King went this morning and the Prince of Orange will be at Oxford this night.'

James, however, was not as lucky as his consort; captured before he could set sail, he was taken back to London and the rioting crowds. No one knows whether it was deliberate or not, but lack of vigilance enabled James to flee once more, this time leaving behind a note in which he wrongly forecast the future, predicting that he would return when the nation realized its mistake and allowed liberty of conscience. From his French sanctuary James, who had dropped the Great Seal in the Thames, drafted the reason for his 'withdrawal' and Parliament, sitting in committee, debated whether or not the throne was vacant. Finally the House of Commons resolved 'that King James the Second, having endeavoured to subvert the Kingdom by breaking the original contract between King and people ... and having withdrawn himself out of the Kingdom, has abdicated the government and that the Throne thereby is become vacant'.

At first the House of Lords opposed it, preferring the word 'deserted' to 'abdicated'. But the Lower Chamber was adamant, contending that the sovereign had 'renounced to be a King according to the law – such a King as he swore to be at his coronation ... and had set up another kind of dominion, which is to all intents an abdication'. Acting as a revolutionary convention, both Lords and Commons elected William of Orange and his wife Mary, elder daughter of James II and Anne Hyde, to the throne.

The Glorious Revolution of 1688 had a drastic effect on the monarchy. William III and Mary II ascended the throne conditionally – by accepting the Bill of Rights the following February. This famous document – ranking with Magna Carta as one of the two supreme constitutional documents in English history – declared that the sovereign no longer reigned by divine or pure hereditary right, but by virtue of an Act of Parliament. From that time, whoever occupied the throne would neither be a papist nor be married to one. The Bill inexorably affirmed that anyone 'who shall profess the popish religion, or shall marry a papist, shall be excluded and be for ever incapable to inherit, possess or enjoy the Crown and government of this realm'. The Protestant Church of England and the Protestant monarch were thus united by law. To prevent a sovereign from enjoying a clandestine relationship with Rome yet ostensibly professing the Protestant faith, Parliament introduced an Act of Parliament relating to the coronation oath. This instructed that in the crowning of future monarchs 'the Archbishop of Canterbury shall say: "Will you to the utmost of your power maintain the laws of God, the true provision of the Gospel, and the Protestant Reformed Religion established by law ... ?" '.

The Act of Settlement of 1701, which reinforced the Bill of Rights, meant that while he held to the Catholic faith, Prince James Francis Edward was debarred from the throne. William agreed to recognize the Prince of Wales as his heir, provided that he was sent to England and was loyal to Protestantism. But James and his consort Mary of Modena, in their court at St Germain, declined to entrust their son to the guardianship of 'the Usurper of Our Kingdom' or to endanger his soul. When he was twelve the young Prince rode in state to Notre-Dame to make his first communion. In the following year the waters of Bourbon failed to cure the dying King. From his blood-stained bed he told his tearful son: 'Remember you must never put the crown of England in competition with your eternal salvation. There is no slavery like sin, and no liberty like service to God ... If Providence wills that you shall sit upon the throne of your ancestors ... govern your people with justice and clemency ... Kings are not made for themselves but for the good of all people ... You are the child of vows and prayers. Behave yourself accordingly.'

About an hour later the young Prince, then thirteen, was proclaimed King James III at the gates of St Germain, but he never reigned over an inch of British soil. He might have done so if, like Henry IV of France, he had adopted a religion that was alien to his beliefs, but one that he thought it imperative to acknowledge. But he remained true to Catholicism and it was his Protestant half-sister Anne (daughter of James II and Anne Hyde) who in 1702 succeeded her brother-in-law as Queen. The crown would now pass to the descendants of Sophia, Electress of Hanover, a granddaughter of James I, should Anne die childless.

Now grown to young manhood, James, having attempted to join the Scottish Jacobites (the name given to his supporters), only to be driven back by a superior fleet, tried to persuade Queen Anne of the justice of his cause. 'Surely,' he wrote, 'you will prefer your own brother, the last of our name, to the House of Hanover (the remotest relations we have), whose friendship there is no reason to rely on and who will leave the government to foreigners!' Yet whatever sympathy Anne may have secretly had for the Catholic prince, the support for Hanover prevailed. To the non-Catholics James was the 'Pretender' and not, as the Prince of Wales, the heir to his father's throne.

Yet the cry of 'No Hanover!' had by no means been silenced, and it was greatly due to Jacobite tardiness that James lost his chance to grasp the crown. Queen Anne died in August 1714. The pro-Hanoverians were prepared, the Jacobites were not; lacking a pre-concerted plan, the followers of James bungled the issue at the crucial moment. If they had promptly proclaimed him King, the Catholic Stuarts might have regained the throne. But for some reason they lost the initiative. The Protestant Elector of Hanover, the future George I, who could scarcely speak a word of English, journeyed from Hanover. The Battle of Sheriffmuir was fought, leaving the clans victorious, but they were badly organized and insufficiently united and the 1715 Jacobite rebellion petered out. A price of £100,000 was set on Prince James's head even before he sighted the coast of Scotland.

James returned to France, which now ceased to be a permanent sanctuary, in a fishing-boat and lived successively in Avignon, Florence and finally Rome, relying on a pension from the Pope. He created his elder son Charles Edward Prince of Wales, but the title was as empty as his own. Bonnie Prince Charlie (the 'Young Pretender', whereas his father was known as the 'Old Pretender') would end his days in drunkenness and debauchery in Rome. On his death his younger brother took the ineffectual title of Henry IX, having his medals inscribed *voluntate Dei non hominium* (by the will of God, not of man). Henry, however, was realistic, declining to pine for what was now the impossible. As Cardinal York he rose to be a prince of the Catholic Church and when the French Revolution seriously sapped his revenues he readily accepted a pension from his Hanoverian cousin George III. With his death in 1805 the Stuart claim to the throne was snuffed out.

Through the generosity of George IV, the Old Pretender and his sons were commemorated in the great basilisk of St Peter's in Rome. Protestantism had driven them into tragic exile, for it was solely on religious grounds that the Catholic Stuarts were thrust from the throne. If they had recanted their Catholic faith, Prince Charles would not be the heir apparent today.

Protestantism greatly transformed the royal family, imposing tremendous restraint on them. As we have seen, the Act of Settlement held that the occupant of the throne must be a Protestant; a Catholic was totally banned. In this democratic age, when Anglican churchgoing has dwindled and there is no longer friction between the Church of England and Rome, it can be argued that this provision not only discriminates against Roman Catholics, but offends against the basic human right entitling the monarch to have liberty of religious thought. In theory all this may be valid, but in practice, as one writer has pointed out, 'the relation of Crown and Church is the course of history, not logic'. Therefore while the sovereign retains royal supremacy over the Church as its supreme governor, compulsory membership of the Church of England is neither an unreasonable nor an inappropriate condition of kingship. Moreover while the Church of England continues to be linked with the state it is preferable that, since most people claim to be Protestants, the sovereign should not be separated from the majority of his or her subjects. Thus before any restriction on the sovereign's religion can be removed, the Church must divest itself entirely of its state connection.

But what of the future? One of the Queen's religious advisers is on record as saying that Prince Charles is 'very keen to see the reformation of the Church. Within the next fifty years, the Protestant church will be united and the Roman Catholic and Anglican Churches will be restyled. Even the monarchy will have a chance to liberate itself from the past. Charles is very aware of this.' Considering, however, that on 8 July 1969 the convocations of Canterbury and York refused to unite with the Methodist Church, this may be baseless optimism. But no one knows what the future holds.

In the meantime Prince Charles has revealed no tendency to rebel because, as heir apparent, the law deprives him of liberty of conscience. He has found himself naturally bound to the Anglican Church, whose tolerance has also enabled him to respect the tenets and practices of the Church of Scotland. He was confirmed at Easter 1965 by the Archbishop of Canterbury at Windsor, having received instruction from the Dean of Windsor. Charles's brand of religion, in common with that of other members of the royal family, has been defined as 'Prayer Book Anglicanism'; that is, neither High nor Low Church. Like the Queen and George VI, the Prince of Wales has a sincere feeling for religion. When at Windsor he is a frequent communicant, rising early on weekdays as well as Sundays to walk from the quadrangle to St George's Chapel.

Within months of the Prince's confirmation there occurred the most momentous event in his life so far : his eighteenth birthday. There is a widespread belief that members of the royal family have always come of age when eighteen, though there has never been a shred of legal backing for this. By the law of the land, only the monarch is always of age. Thus until the change in the law everyone else, regardless of rank, was a minor until the age of twenty-one. Now all minors legally come of age at eighteen.

Under the Regency Act of 1953, however, Charles could reign without a regent on the abdication or death of the Queen. Moreover, should the Queen be temporarily incapable of fulfilling her duties, he would discharge them as regent. Thus in that capacity he replaced Prince Philip, perhaps to the gratification of certain Tories. The Act had broken away from tradition, away from the hereditary right whereby the next senior member in the succession served – should the need arise – as regent. In this case it was Princess Margaret who ranked immediately after the Queen's children. There had been a precedent even in the previous reign. Under the Regency Act of 1937, the Duke of Gloucester would have been regent if George VI had died before Princess Elizabeth reached her eighteenth birthday. But now the hereditary principle was to be abandoned : Princess Margaret would be replaced by Prince Philip, her brother-in-law, who was distinctly remote in the line of succession from the throne. The reason given for this departure from tradition was a father's right to be responsible for the rearing of his son – a guardianship that was pinpointed in the Queen's message to Parliament. Read by the Home Secretary, Sir David Maxwell Fyfe, it said : 'The uncertainty of human life leads me to put you in mind of the possibility that a child of myself and my dear husband may succeed to the throne whilst under the age of eighteen years. And I would recommend to your consideration whether it be no expediency to provide that, in that event and also in the event of a Regency becoming necessary during my lifetime, whilst there is no child or grandchild of ours who can be the Regent, my husband should be the Regent and be charged with the guardianship of the person of the Sovereign.'

Misgivings lurked in some Tory minds, however. By now the romance of Princess Margaret and Group Captain Peter Townsend, the late King's equerry, was common knowledge. There was nothing to prevent the marriage, even though the Group Captain was a divorcee, but the Princess would have had to renounce her royal rights. Strident echoes of the abdication crisis of 1936 now made themselves heard. Sympathizers of the Duke of Windsor hinted at a link between Margaret's desire to marry and the move to amend the Regency Act of 1937. Secret undercurrents of resentment towards Philip himself also came to the surface. He was depicted as the outspoken alien prince, a Battenberg, arrogantly meddling with the constitution.

In fact there was no connection; the timing of the Bill was determined solely by the forthcoming Commonwealth tour, which had been twice postponed because of the late King's illness. The Chancellor of the Exchequer, R. A. Butler (who as Lord Butler would be Charles's mentor at Cambridge), pleaded in the House of Commons for a cessation of 'deplorable speculation'. The Bill was passed, leaving Prince Philip as a potential regent and empowering the Queen Mother, who was herself distant in the line of succession, to be a Councillor of State.

The 1937 Regency Act had created an irregularity: whereas Princess Elizabeth could have assumed sovereign powers at eighteen, she was precluded from taking up the minor office of Councillor of State until she was twenty-one. Six years elapsed before this anomaly was put right. As a result of this change, at his eighteenth birthday Prince Charles became both a potential regent and a Councillor of State.

Despite his new and exalted station, Prince Charles's eighteenth birthday was little different from any other day at Gordonstoun. The Court Circular issued from Buckingham Palace merely announced unostentatiously: 'Today is the Anniversary of the Birthday of the Prince of Wales.' Charles rose as usual at about seven o'clock, then adhered to the normal routine. Only the greetings cards, the telephone conversations with other members of the royal family and a coffee party for some friends after studies at nine that night made the day any different from the rest. In London the judges at the Central Criminal Court donned their scarlet robes as a gesture to the future king, and during the evening the bells rang out over Windsor from the ancient Curfew Tower.

One privilege granted to the Prince on his eighteenth birthday was financial. Fourteen years earlier, at the Queen's accession, he had automatically assumed the title of Duke of Cornwall. With it went the assets of the duchy whose net revenues are the traditional inheritance of the heir apparent. By arrangement with the Treasury, only £15,000 of the total annual income was taken by the Queen for her son's education and future needs; the remainder was set against the civil list – the budget granted by Parliament to the monarch at the beginning of his or her reign in return for the income from the crown estates. Now that he was eighteen, the figure would be doubled to £30,000, but it would still be paid to the Queen on the Prince's behalf. Not until he was twenty-one would he himself be entitled to the total revenue. As a report in *The Times* of 26 August 1969 revealed, when that time arrived the Prince had decided that he would surrender half of the income to which he was then entitled; the remainder would be allocated to the Consolidated Fund – in short, to the Exchequer. Because the total net revenue today is in the region of £220,000, Prince Charles receives about £110,000 each year tax free. The arrangement can, however, be reviewed should the Prince get married or circumstances change.

Many people think that sums were being amassed during the Prince's minority, a false impression that Mr P. G. T. Kingsley, secretary of the Duchy of Cornwall, felt bound to correct in a report in the *Daily Telegraph* of 24 October 1958:

'Some of you [the tenants of the Duchy] may have read quite recently one such article which told of the income of the Prince of Wales piling up during the minority, and that it had, in fact, been piling up for twenty years since the last Prince of Wales came to the throne as Edward VIII. I have no objection to fairy tales, but one must distinguish between fact and fiction. So I think it might be of interest in this connection to tell you that, except for a small proportion which is retained for the benefit of the Prince of Wales, dues of the Duchy go to the relief of the Civil List by the Queen.'

The civil list originated in the reign of William and Mary. They were granted £600,000 to defray expenses of the royal household, the maintenance of palaces and gardens, the salaries of the judges, ambassadors and civil servants, and pensions. (The cost of defending the nation was excluded.) This system remained fundamentally the same in subsequent reigns. For this purpose the sovereign had available hereditary revenues made up of income from crown lands and other sources such as prerogative rights in treasure trove, royal mines, fish and swans, and from certain ecclesiastical sources such as tithes or the income of bishoprics during a vacancy. Parliament also granted the monarch the income from some customs duties, from certain taxes (for example, those on beer, ale and cider) and the post office revenues. When Britain's population grew, the cost of government increased commensurately and income from all sources proved inadequate. Thus George III allowed Parliament to retain most of the hereditary revenues and received in return an annual grant (civil list) of £800,000. This in turn became insufficient and in 1830 the extraneous charges on the civil list were removed and the amount of the grant was reduced. But in those times of war, acute poverty and social and industrial change George III – and later his son George IV – did well out of the deal. The prodigality of the fourth George, whose adulterous escapades and gambling debts were notorious, persuaded Parliament to grant him an additional £500,000. In return he yielded all the hereditary dues of England (other than those of the Duchies of Lancaster and Cornwall) and Wales. In the next reign William IV also yielded the revenues of Ireland.

Cornwall had been an earldom from at least 1140. Richard, King of the Romans, younger brother of Henry III, was the first royal earl, and when his son Edmund died without heirs, Edward II gave the dignity to his detested favourite, Piers Gaveston. On the latter's murder in 1312 the earldom reverted to the crown. Edward III conferred it on his younger brother, Lord John of Eltham, who died childless in 1334. Three years later, on 17 March 1337, the King created the Dukedom and Duchy of Cornwall, bestowing it on his eldest son, the Black Prince, then six years old. Edward's charter, which is still extant in the British Museum, was read to Parliament, expressing with unmistakable clarity both to his own age and to posterity the King's intentions: 'To have and to hold to the same Duke and first begotten sons of him and his heirs, being Kings of England and Dukes of Cornwall by succession of inheritance.'

Selden claimed: 'By this creation not only was the first-born son of the Kings of England, but the eldest living also are always Dukes of Cornwall.' It should be stressed that only the sovereign's first-

born or eldest surviving son can inherit the title – a daughter may
never do so, even though she may be next in line to the throne. That
is why the Queen, as Princess Elizabeth, could never qualify; instead the dukedom and the duchy's revenues temporarily reverted
to the crown. For nearly half the time of the title's long existence,
the crown has enjoyed its revenues because there was no duke.

Obviously Prince Charles inherited his title only at his mother's
accession. Since then, as the premier royal duke, he has been head
of the nation's peerage. During his minority the privileges and
authorities invested in the Duke under the Duchy of Cornwall
Amendment Acts 1863 to 1893 were exercised by the Queen (as her
son's guardian), who appointed and presided over a council of nine.

For more than six centuries Edward III's time-honoured trust has
been assailed at times, but the principle of properties reverting to
the duchy or to the crown has been upheld. A precedent was established even on the death of the first duke. On occasions the Black
Prince was generous in rewarding gallantry and services in times of
war, but when he died the new owners of the properties and land
concerned were compelled to return them. Thus gratitude was relatively short lived, for whatever the circumstances in which the
title-holders might wish to dispose of parts of the ducal demesne,
they were eventually restored. Even the lands sold by Cromwell
during the Commonwealth were bought back when Charles II was
restored to the throne. Thus the duchy revenues were not whittled
away.

But whether sovereign or title-holder, most royal landlords were
absentees, looking upon their vast estates as lucrative revenue. A
change of attitude came in the eighteenth century, however. One
can criticize the Hanoverians for much of their behaviour, but they
were apparently the first to show any real interest in the duchy's
tenants. George IV had an additional interest: to defray some of his
enormous debts, he allowed the banker Thomas Coutts to receive
the revenues during his – the King's – lifetime. In effect this celebrated banker in London's Strand was the Duke of Cornwall for a
time. (Incidentally the royal family have continued the association
with the bank that Coutts made famous, their cheques being no
different from those in common use apart from specific monograms
surmounted by a crown or coronet.)

Over the years duchy revenues have taken a variety of forms. In
the Middle Ages, for instance, the feudal system prevailed: tenants

paid their rent in kind or in military service. Tenants were categorized in three groups: natives of stock who depended on the various lords of the manor for their properties; free conventionary tenants; and native conventionary tenants. Conditions of tenure were very restricting. In the duchy's earliest years, in the reign of its creator Edward III, a native of stock agreed to surrender his chattels to his lord at his death, 'and his last-born shall have the land by fine [key money] ... and he shall not send his son to school nor marry his daughter, without licence of the lord'. With these complexities, people's lives must have depended substantially on the whims of the local lord, and perhaps many sighed with relief when such legal agreements ended in the days of Elizabeth I. Conventionary tenants also experienced some limitations. As a rule tenancies were held for a mere seven years and to renew the lease the tenant was compelled to apply to courts of assession. Whatever the merits or demerits of these legal contracts, they operated until the middle of the nineteenth century.

The most intriguing rents were those in kind: they might take the form of a quantity of pepper, roses, even a solitary red rose or a grain of wheat. More sophisticated was a pair of gilt spurs – the due of a certain lord of the manor – whereas the Lord of Elerk's commitment was a greyhound. A visit from the royal landlord was a time for ritual. One tenant welcomed the duke with a bow and twelve arrows; another was obliged to bake him a pie of raisins, limpets and herbs; others bore grey cloth capes ahead of him for forty days. In the Scilly Isles the annual rent comprised three hundred puffins, but by the reign of Henry VI the due had been reduced to fifty puffins or 6s 8d.

When Edward III founded England's first dukedom and duchy, his object was to guarantee an income for the heir apparent. Apart from the Duchy of Lancaster, which the same Edward granted in 1362 to his third son, John of Gaunt, subsequent dukedoms were not duchies with domains. On the Black Prince's creation as Duke of Cornwall Cornish castles at Tintagel, Launceston and Restormel, as well as Trematon, Maiden and Liskeard, including their boroughs and manors, went with the dukedom. In the neighbouring county of Devon the castle at Exeter and the manor and borough of Lydford were added, as were similar estates and grants of land in other parts of England. It did not end there: a second charter – also of 1337 – absorbed the manors of Vauxhall and Kennington (King's

Town) in Surrey. Dues also came from the mining of tin. The industry had long flourished, and by the end of the twelfth century the Lord Warden of the Stannaries was second in status only to the sovereign in the West Country. Derived from the Latin word *stannum*, meaning tin, the Stannaries comprised mine-working areas such as Blackmore and Truro. A profitable industry enabled the mines to amass power, and they even formulated their own laws and controlled their own parliament (which ceased in the mideighteenth century) and court (the jurisdiction of which was abolished in 1896).

Tin-mining no longer thrives but other sources have been – and in some instances continue to be – tapped for revenue: coal, clay and china clay and fuller's earth, flowers, vegetables and Dartmoor peat. Oyster fisheries have contributed too, and for more than six hundred years cider apple-growing has gone unbroken at Bradninch Manor.

It was not until Queen Victoria's reign, however, that the duchy's assets were placed on a business-like basis. Prince Albert discovered, for instance, that in the case of some properties, after the payment of the initial fine, or key money, the duchy had received no further revenue during the lives of three consecutive tenants. The Prince Consort systematically pruned anomalies. In particular, because of his acumen the Kennington estate grew extremely profitable. The Prince Consort was not only far-sighted but also an innovator, pioneering the erection of flats along that stretch of the Thames embankment that was christened after him. It set a standard for the future, for the new properties that the duchy and former London County Council built jointly were to rehouse many tenants from demolished slums.

The future Edward VII had good reason to be grateful to the Consort, who managed the duchy during his son's minority. To his delight Edward discovered that the revenues yielded him an annual income of £50,000, a substantial sum in those times. Dues had been wisely invested and from a fund of £600,000 Edward bought for £220,000 the estate that gave him so much pleasure – Sandringham. The duchy that Prince Charles inherited is vast. He is the landlord of properties in Cornwall, Dorset, Somerset, Wiltshire, Berkshire and London, though Vauxhall, once noted for its gardens and a favourite haunt of Regency London, is no longer part of the duchy. Today's better-known tenancies include Kennington Oval, the set-

ting of Surrey and Test cricket, and Dartmoor and its prison at
Princetown, for which Charles receives rent.

Dartmoor tenants – clergymen, innkeepers and farmers – are
notoriously loyal to their royal landlord. Happily, in 1952 – when
the Prince succeeded to the ducal title on his mother's accession –
they could again, after a lapse of fifteen years, toast another Duke
of Cornwall. At their annual dinner at Two Bridges they did so in
ale. They paid their dues and smoked their allotment of tobacco in
the traditional churchwarden pipes supplied to them. Then they
wrote to the Queen: 'All tenants of His Royal Highness the Duke
of Cornwall on Dartmoor attending the annual audit dinner today
join in sending with their humble duty this expression of their
loyalty to your Majesty and to their Royal landlord.'

Before the First World War about £300,000 was allocated to improve the estates. Gross receipts were then some £130,000 each
year, and by the 1930s they had amounted to about £215,000. This
was a sizeable income, enabling Edward VIII, who retained the
revenues since there was no Duke of Cornwall, to grant an allowance to his brother Prince Albert from duchy funds. On ascending
the throne as George VI, Albert in turn guaranteed an income to his
brother, the Duke of Gloucester. The Queen and Prince Philip have
continued to consolidate and improve on what was done before
them, so that today Prince Charles is the landlord of almost 140,000
acres and some thousands of tenants. Typical of the progressive attitude in the duchy is the Stoke Climsland model farm in Cornwall –
the latest development in agriculture – which allows tenant farmers
to improve the quality of their livestock; and a lucrative flower industry, which includes laboratories for the study of bulb diseases. In
1959 the duchy was augmented by the acquisition of 12,500 acres –
the Daglingworth estate near Cirencester in Gloucestershire. The
transaction also includes a private school for boys. Prince Charles
therefore owns a school, as well as paying the fees at Gordonstoun
for a boy chosen from the duchy.

Instead of disintegrating over the centuries, the duchy today is a
model of financial prudence administered by the Lord Warden of
the Stannaries, the Keeper of the Privy Seal, the Attorney-General,
the Receiver General, the Keeper of the Records and other officials
of a headquarters staff housed in a mansion in Birdcage Walk near
Buckingham Palace.

Modern business techniques are not, however, allowed to override ancient customs such as the simple annual ceremonies held at the manor of Fordington in Dorset, which was granted to the Black Prince by charter on 9 July 1342. On St George's Day the locals roast a sheep and the vicar dispatches a leg by post to Prince Charles as rent for the annual fair. The rest of the sheep is auctioned for charity. With unfailing regularity the villagers also haul an oak bough to the top of the church on 29 May – Oak Apple Day. No one seems to know how the customs originated, but tradition dies hard.

Prince Charles inherited his Scottish titles as the monarch's eldest son because he is the heir to the old kingdom of Scotland. These were the titles brought to the English court by Prince Henry when his father, James VI of Scotland, succeeded Elizabeth I as James I of England. The title of Great Steward of Scotland goes far back into Scottish history. Charles's Stewart ancestor was High Steward of Scotland and it was his issue who became Kings of Scotland. Marjorie, the daughter of the great Robert the Bruce, married Walter, the sixth High Steward of Scotland. Their son was crowned Robert II, and from him sprang the royal dynasty of Stewart.

One title that recalls just as graphically Scotland's past – certainly some of its more violent moments – is that of Lord of the Isles. It refers to the rugged isles off the country's western coast. In medieval times the title-holders led the Clan Donald and, like John, son of Og, who in 1354 took the title of *Dominus Insularum*, they resented paying homage to the King of Scots. Scorning allegiance, they conducted their affairs independently as separate sovereigns. But their own treachery destroyed them. The clan entered into a treaty with England's Edward IV to conquer Scotland. The Donald spoils would comprise the northern Highlands, and the Earl of Douglas would also enlarge his territory. Edward was to be the overlord of the remainder. But the plot misfired: the intrigue reached the ears of the Scots King, who compelled the Lord of the Isles to forfeit territory to the crown and pay homage. The Lord of the Isles had been self-styled, but after 1476 the title was placed on a feudal basis and could be withdrawn. That was precisely its fate during a further rebellious outbreak. In 1493 it was confiscated by the King of the Scots.

9 This Feeling of Duty

Whereas the monarch has always symbolized the nation as a whole, the heir apparent has been defined as the 'supreme representative' of his generation. It could be argued that Prince Charles is the apotheosis of a far wider cross-section of society. Blessed with an enviable streak of humour in his make-up, he is conscientious and extremely competent in whatever he essays. And always there is that air of assurance. Although it may seem trite in an age when old-fashioned standards are debunked, he has a keen sense of honour, a distinct respect for those older than himself, a frank admiration for tradition and ideals that to some people seem incongruous in today's rebellious society. The fact is that, like the Queen and Prince Philip, the Prince of Wales has courage and convictions, refusing to seek cheap popularity by pandering to the inanities admired by many in our current unstable times. His unshakable piety, without sanctimoniousness, his genuine regard for the welfare of others and his awareness of the need to shore up weakening morality are standards to which our materialistic and rather decadent nation would do well to aspire.

Outside the prescribed limitations of constitutional demands, he declines to be anyone's pawn. A notable illustration is his refusal – no doubt to the chagrin and dismay of the tailoring trade – to be a leader of fashion. Although he was still not yet six years old, in April 1954 the *Tailor and Cutter*, which arrogates to itself the right to decide on sartorial standards, lauded the boy-prince as one of the eleven best-dressed men of the year. Perhaps intended as a stimulus to trade, its announcement ran : 'His Baby-Bow and Fawn Stalkers, followed by his junior fashion for a double-breasted woolly, is accentuated this year by his adoption of a very popular style among older folk. His velvet-collared topcoat also follows a popular current trend.' A rash of little velvet-collared topcoats was noted. But Prince Charles has since failed to fulfil the hopes of the trade. Indeed the

Tailor and Cutter later criticized him for his 'cult of studied shabbiness'. Retaliating, Charles arrived at the annual dinner of the Master Tailors' Benevolent Association wearing an old tweed jacket over his white dress shirt. Changing into tails for his speech, he joked: 'I am often asked whether it is because of some generic trait that I stand with my hands behind my back, like my father. The answer is that we both have the same tailor. He makes the sleeves so tight we can't get our hands in front.'

Rightly or wrongly, unlike earlier Princes of Wales he has shown no desire to be an arbiter of fashion. Things were very different in other reigns. Let us take the case of Victoria's heir. When he was only ten years old she wrote to her eldest son: 'Dress is a trifling matter ... But it gives also the one outward sign from which people in general can and often do judge upon the *inward* state of mind and feeling of a person ... we do not wish to control your own tastes and fancies ... but we do *expect* that you will never wear anything *extravagant* or *slang*.' In the Queen's view clothes made the prince in the eyes of the people. Prince Albert Edward emerged as the best-dressed prince, rivalling his foppish predecessor, George IV. Commenting on Victoria's dictum, the Duke of Windsor (who himself influenced sartorial styles) wondered whether or not in the eyes of 'certain sections of the Press I was not more of a glorified clothes-peg than the heir apparent. Nevertheless, my great-grandmother's homily expresses sentiments with which I cordially agree.'

Times have certainly changed. The Prince Consort even issued a paper 'for the guidance of gentlemen appointed to attend on the Prince of Wales'. 'A gentleman', he emphasized in his strait-laced fashion, 'does not indulge in careless, self-indulgent, lounging ways, such as lolling in armchairs, or on sofas, slouching in his gait ... He will borrow nothing from the fashion of the groom or the game-keeper.' Yet having accepted his parents' injunction, Prince Albert Edward was rebuked by the Prince Consort when he was seventeen years old. 'Unfortunately,' he told the Princess Royal, 'he takes no interest in anything but clothes, and again clothes. Even when out shooting he is more occupied with his trousers than with the game.' As for the Consort, when he himself went shooting he wore a black velvet jacket and long scarlet boots. To the Queen he was 'very picturesque', but the British gentry, according to Lytton Strachey, thought the Consort looked 'more like some foreign tenor'.

The son did, however, adopt his father's innovation of wearing a velvet jacket, combining it with velvet trousers for wear in country houses. As Prince of Wales (and later as King) Albert Edward had a wider influence on masculine fashion than any member of the royal family since George IV. 'He was a good friend to the tailors of Savile Row,' wrote the Duke of Windsor, 'consolidating the position of London as the international sartorial shrine for men ... When he visited Marienbad ... tailors from Paris, Vienna and all parts of the Continent used to gather and to follow him around, surreptitiously photographing him and jotting down notes on his clothes.' Once, at the theatre, he was so impressed by a French actor's coat – 'a mass of rents and patches' – that, after the curtain fell, he sent for him to ask the name of his tailor. 'Poole,' came the reply, and from that moment Poole became the Prince's chief tailor.

Albert Edward was one of the first to introduce a crease in his trousers, and to wear a low-cut white waistcoat with a dress-coat; he also helped to popularize a bowler hat, although the *Tailor and Cutter* denounced this as 'an abomination in head gear'. The Prince favoured a grey bowler for summer wear and also wore a brown one that captured the fancy of Americans. From Germany he brought back the Homburg hat, which had intrigued him in a felt factory in Homburg.

Royalty can have a far-reaching influence on fashions, as the Duke of Windsor once explained: 'My father's tartan suit ... began to influence fashions ... half a century after it was made in the eighteen-nineties. I happened to wear it one evening for dinner at La Croe near Antibes ... One of our guests mentioned the fact to a friend in the men's fashion trade, who immediately cabled the news to America. Within a few months tartan had become a popular material for every sort of masculine garment, from dinner jackets and cummerbunds to swimming-trunks and beach shorts. Later the craze even extended to luggage.'

Doubtless Prince Charles could himself be a trend-setter – with a subsequent impact on trade – but so far he has rejected everything that smacks of the jet-set, adopting instead conventional standards, as is clear from his quiet, traditional clothes. In so doing he has gained rather than lost popularity in times when many of his contemporaries often prefer the bizarre. Maybe it is his air of ordinariness, despite the background of hereditary splendour (and the international curiosity that he somehow attracts), that has won him widespread public acceptance.

Yet because of the royal status and its magnetism for the media, a great strain has been imposed upon him. Student stress, for instance, is a complaint of modern times, yet Prince Charles was expected to cope not only with the pressures of undergraduate life but also with interruptions in the guise of official duties. In addition, a whole summer term was spent at the University College of Wales with its disconcerting threats and danger. There was also the constant reminder that whatever he said or did might quickly become public knowledge, and be distorted for good or ill. In the clutter of undergraduate bicycles at Cambridge it would always be his – and its rider – that was photographed. For most people to imagine themselves under this relentless public microscope is daunting; to accept it and yet avoid having one's innate qualities impaired seems impossible.

Prince Charles, however, has accomplished this feat with the skill of someone of riper years. Not for him the luxury of anonymity. His most casual word becomes a public utterance. His simplest action is a topic for the international press. He could not even search for scrumpy cider in Okehampton in peace and quiet. Because the incident occurred in the Duchy of Cornwall, he was instantly recognized. 'Marvellous old boys in caps,' he recalled, 'came up and said: "Like ter shake yer 'and." They were charming. One old boy produced his Home Guard certificate signed by my grandfather. But that sort of thing never gets reported. It was all this business of looking for scrumpy. Everyone must think I'm an alcoholic.'

Charles can go nowhere as a private person, only as the Prince of Wales. Disguise is pointless. He attempted it once as a Cambridge student. Curious to witness a demonstration, he borrowed an overcoat, raised the collar and pulled a hat down over his eyes. But it was useless. 'I just looked like me trying not to look like me. Everybody kept looking. Wearing dark glasses was just as ineffectual,' he added. '. . . everyone wonders what on earth you are doing wearing dark glasses, particularly when the sun is not out. Even if you put on a false beard . . . it will blow away.'

It was precisely this sort of disguise that the rather sensational *France Dimanche* claimed the Prince of Wales was affecting. Donning a false black beard, they reported, the royal 'phantom' travelled incognito to visit a young lady in Fulham. Charles has long since resigned himself to the antics and fabrications of the 'incredibly disreputable' foreign newspapers. He knows that many people are avid to read such things even if – somewhat ridiculously – they realize they are nonsense, adding philosophically: 'Anyway the time to get anxious . . . is when nobody is interested at all.'

Rather in the style of Prince Philip, the Prince of Wales has the facility to mingle with all types of people within the community, a valuable asset in public life. To some people his approach may appear to be contrived, the outcome of studious calculation. But this is not so. Prince Charles is drawn instinctively to theatricals and, as in the case of an actor, he is both himself and the role he happens to portray. But there the analogy ends. There is no rehearsal or performance; it is perfectly natural. Many in such a position would be tempted to be circumspect, thinking twice before any action or remark. But the Prince has candour and, seemingly, whether this is serious or humorous, lacks inhibition. He does everything with the right degree of timing.

Typical was the evening when he made the mistake of arriving in a dinner jacket at an Edinburgh function, while the rest of the gathering wore white ties and tails. 'I do not know what you are doing,' he apologized with cheerful confidence, 'all dressed like butlers.' Many people find his humour his most engaging trait. Until he exploded on the world in a memorable radio interview in 1969, relatively few people knew of, or even suspected, this flair for humour. Up to that time ordinary people had been regaled on Fleet Street trivia.

Prince Charles does not possess the wit of Prince Philip, but humour is preferable in a future monarch, for in wit there is often a leavening of acrimony. A story is told of the time when Prince Charles was the main speaker at a naval commander-in-chief's dinner. Complaining that souvenir hunters had deprived him of more naval caps than any sailor since Nelson, he said that he strongly suspected that the offenders were visiting Australian Navy officers on board. 'And so,' he announced solemnly, 'I got on the 'phone to Mum to ask her advice as a good son should. I asked her if I could have the culprits thrown into the Tower. "Of course, my boy," she told me. "The sooner the better. For one thing, the replacement of uniforms is proving costly for the crown." And so I propose to act on my mother's advice.' Charles then blew hard on a whistle and the Master-of-Arms burst in followed by naval police. After they had hustled the Australians out of the wardroom a volley of shots was heard. The Australians lay on the deck in pants and singlets covered in tomato sauce.

An inveterate practical joker, the Prince threatened officers with the Tower on a round-the-world voyage in HMS *Jupiter*. When the ship returned to Plymouth a black minibus drew alongside her bearing the words: 'HM Tower of London for officers of HMS *Jupiter*.' Again, while Charles was swimming in the tropics near the eight-year-old son of a fellow officer, the boy asked 'What's your name?' 'Charles,' came the reply, 'but a lot of people call me Charlie.' 'You aren't Charles, the Prince?' queried the boy. 'Well, yes, I am. But you see I can't wear my crown in the water.'

The royal jokes have been known to brighten up a boring meeting or even to calm irate discussion. Such an instance occurred when he presided over a conference on industry and the environment. For some while conservationists, industrialists, trade-union leaders and students had been arguing passionately, so that by the time the Prince rose to speak the atmosphere was quite strained. To have made the wrong remark would have been inflammatory, exposing the Prince to widespread public ridicule. Instead tempers cooled and anger turned to laughter when he began: 'As the bishop said to the actress, this thing is bigger than both of us.'

Yet again, on unveiling a bust of Prince Philip at the Royal Thames Yacht Club, he commented: 'Not that I am accustomed in any way to unveiling busts', and added at the actual unveiling: 'I now complete the process of helping my father to expose himself.'

The Prince does not, however, escape the occasional blunder. While planting a tree for the Prince of Wales Committee in Wales, he expressed delight that it was an oak-tree – 'and not one of those ghastly spruces'. Forestry workers who planted spruces up and down Britain were quickly incensed and in pacifying the Forestry Commission, the advocates of the oak tree were just as displeased.

Prince Charles has learnt that the royal route is strewn with thorns as well as flowers. But his amiability helps him to accept in-anities with a measure of humility and common sense. This quality, supported by quiet self-confidence, insures him against any resentment. To some extent the self-assurance is born of the knowledge that deference is paid to him as the future king. Consequently on being launched into public life, he found it easier at first to deal with public engagements rather than private ones: in the former his role was rigidly defined, but on private occasions people were often hesitant in reacting to him, and he often encountered extremes of behaviour in otherwise normal people.

That was a drawback when he joined the Royal Air Force and then the Navy. The dual standards cropped up again : he was a mere sub-lieutenant in Service rank, yet no one could ignore that he was also the Prince of Wales. For Charles this situation necessitated considerable resourcefulness. Somehow it was assumed that he would excel. There was no question about it. So when he secured his RAF pilot's wings in a shorter time than was normally allowed, this was only to be expected. When he parachuted into the English Channel his feat was taken for granted. A shortened course of introduction and a reduced period of training confronted him in the Royal Navy, compelling him to assimilate a considerable amount of technical and navigational data more quickly than anyone else. 'The trouble', he once mildly protested, 'is that people expect one to be a genius ... and to achieve the impossible rather sooner than in the immediate.'

Prince Charles was happy and accomplished in his career as a naval pilot. The variety of duties it offered – community flying, rocket firing and alighting on carriers or the sterns of ships (maybe in a fierce gale) – injected his life with excitement and gusto. He has proved himself in whatever sphere he has attempted to enter. Because of the long naval tradition of the royal family, it was not surprising when Prince Charles was appointed captain of the wooden-hulled mine-sweeper HMS *Bronington*.

King George V was convinced that a spell in the Royal Navy was to be recommended for helping the heir to emerge from the chrysalis to kingship. Charles himself endorses this sentiment : 'A period in the Services gives you a greater experience and responsibility of life, of discipline, and above all of people and how to deal with people, to discipline them, and to be disciplined by them.' But a naval career must inevitably be limited; by tradition, as the monarch's understudy he is expected to involve himself in public tasks. But what can these be? In due course one role for which the Prince would be abundantly fitted is that of governor-general. Nowadays the governments of Australia, Canada and New Zealand accept no one in this office but their own nationals. It is improbable, however, that they would reject Prince Charles as the representative of the Queen. Certainly he is the only Englishman who could ever hope to win approval.

Charles himself has an unwavering faith in the Commonwealth's potentialities. In an interview published in the London *Observer*, he explained that as a result of his tours he is conscious 'of a kind of family atmosphere', regardless of colour or creed. 'People seem to feel, or act as though they feel, without being very articulate about it that they've got something – well, in common. Perhaps family atmosphere isn't the accurate way of putting it; but it's the kind of atmosphere you feel most of all in a family ... common experiences, shared traditions and heritages.' However this forward-looking Prince wisely asserts that the Commonwealth,

'... like so many other institutions – like the monarchy – will be what we make of it. If you believe in what it can do, you can make it do things. Its great possibilities are inherent in the fact that it is something which is more ideal than it is material. That can be said of the United Nations too, I suppose, but the Commonwealth, within its capacity, can be more effective because there are ties within it of a kind which do not exist within the UN – ties of common language, culture, experience and history. Meetings of Commonwealth Prime Ministers, Commonwealth associations of lawyers, doctors, and other professions, the Commonwealth Parliamentary Union – all make the Commonwealth a living institution.

'But again [he emphasized] it comes back to the question not only of what the Commonwealth ... does, but also of what we can get it to do, through existing functions and connections – if we want to.'

With far greater perspicacity than many people in maturity possess, Prince Charles warns that the bond between the present generation of Commonwealth leaders will not necessarily last. The next generation of leaders, especially 'in the "black republican parts" will be different men brought up in a different age ... how well we shall got on with that generation will depend on the efforts we put into our relations with this one and how much the Commonwealth institutions appeal to the new generation'.

In comparing the Commonwealth with the EEC, Prince Charles sees the drive behind Commonwealth relations as one of sentiment; the drive behind the European relationship is more practical in character, to do with economics and defence. 'I would put it this way: much as I love Europe and love being a European – after all, I have plenty of European blood in my veins – what impresses me most about Europeans is the way we differ from one another, whereas what impresses me about the Commonwealth is how much, in spite of everything, we have in common.'

It is universally recognized that the sovereign is the lynch-pin of the Commonwealth, and all the more so at a time of loosening ties. In a wider sphere, the royal family is unquestionably the nation's foremost ambassadorial team. No prime minister or group of politicians can match their skill in creating a favourable atmosphere and kindling interest in things British. This is acutely manifest in the Queen's state and other visits, or in the Duke of Edinburgh's sallies abroad to win markets for British exports. The visit of the Queen and Prince Philip to Mexico – to cite just one example – acted as a stimulus to Anglo-Mexican trade.

The energies and undoubted talents of Prince Charles can also be exploited in this direction. His potential was demonstrated during his stay in Japan. A casual talk with the chairman of a mammoth industrial corporation, during which the Prince eulogized the skills and sound workmanship of the Welsh, resulted in a factory being built in South Wales two years later.

Charles, as Prince of Wales, is especially anxious to enrich the life of the Welsh, an aspiration that mirrors a facet of his forceful and uncomplicated character. It is rather incongruous that although he is Prince of Wales he does not own a single item in the principality. Despite this deficiency, he has no intention of letting the title be meaningless. It is his inflexible rule not to identify himself with an association or relationship unless he can 'make it real, productive and as effective as possible'. He recognizes that Welsh resentment of English apathy and arrant neglect has festered into open nationalism. Since the mid-eighteenth century any reference to England in parliamentary legislation has been arrogantly assumed to embrace Wales as well. This situation has irritated and even embittered the Welsh – 'a proud people, and Wales does seem far more to Welshmen than England does to some Englishmen'. The Prince is convinced that this was the forcing-bed for the seeds of Welsh nationalism, to which he was subjected as an English Prince of Wales at Aberystwyth.

With characteristic sympathy and tolerance, he appreciated the prickly reaction of some Welshmen; it was embarrassing but he could understand it. As a young man of action, he grappled with the problem in a practical manner that the politicians might profitably emulate; at personal risk, he courageously mingled with the people in the streets and the public-houses, exhibiting a genuine concern for the Welsh and their problems. Bitterness melted under his cordiality and obvious sincerity and 'a bit of the hot air has gone out of some of the more negative forms of Welsh nationalism'.

To the Prince of Wales it is a question of human relationships, a cardinal ingredient in modern society, but one that has been submerged in the technical age. Prince Charles has been intrigued by human relationships since he was first entrusted with men's welfare and their careers in the Royal Navy. Honesty and personal involvement (flavoured with humour) is his recipe for leadership. Maybe it is an old-fashioned attitude, but it would help to halt the rot in the fabric of present-day society due to a great degree to duplicity and trickery, greed and materialism.

What the politicians have consistently failed to do for Wales the Prince is keen to rectify. His predecessor, the Duke of Windsor, was impregnated with a similar enthusiasm; David Lloyd George, the Prime Minister, had encouraged him to travel at home and abroad, assuring him that personal acquaintance would endear him to his future people. What he had witnessed in the principality – the unemployment, hunger and misery, particularly in the valleys of South Wales – had shocked him. Buoyed up by pseudo-promises, the people – especially the young – had believed themselves to be poised on the edge of a glorious new world. Instead they found themselves in a morass of despair. On his return from Wales the Duke was overwhelmed by frustration and helplessness. Wales, it seemed, was doomed.

There is no parallel today with the tragic twenties and thirties, yet under their resilient Prince and his progressive Prince of Wales Committee, the Welsh are planning for a more productive future. The Committee is Charles's vehicle for translating his ideas for the betterment of urban and rural life. To this young man of ideas tourism is a rich vein to be worked. He recognizes that the Welsh must invest in facilities that are calculated to attract visitors. To stimulate enterprise he proposed to offer prizes and awards for the best hotels and caravan parks and, with the collaboration of the Design Council, for well-designed souvenirs. By motivating people themselves, he has already achieved a great deal without resorting to local or central government. In recent years firms and businesses have rallied to the scheme voluntarily. Other duties are for the moment inevitably curtailing the Prince's activities, but he nurses the ambition that one day 'I can do this sort of thing throughout the country'.

With the spreading of nationalism, it is not inconceivable that parliaments will one day function in Wales and Scotland. (Such a situation would roll back the years to the time when the Welsh and the Scots resisted English conquest.) In that case the holder of titles in both these countries might well become identified with these assemblies. But whatever the Prince endeavours to do, it will be achieved solely through influence. But as Lord Beaconsfield, the redoubtable Disraeli, once declared: 'The most powerful men are not public men. The public man is responsible and the responsible man is a slave. It is a private life that governs the world.' While Prince Charles is obviously a public figure, constitutionally he lacks power; influence is the only instrument by which he can accomplish anything and, as he admits, his influence is in direct ratio to the respect people have for him. If he had any political influence it would have to be clandestine. A former Prince of Wales, the future Edward VII, certainly tried to use his influence in politics, and when he became King he is credited with having surreptitiously prevented the House of Lords from rejecting the Deceased Wife's Sister Bill of 1907. If this is true, it must be the last recorded occasion on which a British sovereign has openly aided the passage of legislation.

To depend on personal popularity for exerting influence may be somewhat precarious, urging caution in the choice of causes that the Prince supports. For instance, he has given as his reason for his association with the Royal Anthropological Society: '... the stronger and more widely influential that organization could be, the better contribution it could make to Britain in facing the problems of a multi-racial society'. His idealistic approach to mass immigration doubtless conflicts with that of many of his countrymen, who would argue that the problem is less anthropological and more numerical.

Whether people agree or disagree with the Prince's views, they cannot ignore the signs of an invigorating leadership that has been notably absent in Britain for some years. Moreover he is willing to adapt to changing times. Since the 1911 investiture, the world has witnessed a fantastic transformation in human affairs. In the foremost countries of Europe and Asia, monarchies have been swept away by cataclysmic upheaval. In Russia, Germany and Austria, in Italy, Turkey and China, once-powerful dynasties are no more than names in history. In China, and more so in the Soviet Union, tyranny has continued to enslave the people, reducing many millions to bondage to pursue sinister aims. Today communism, with its total rejection of monarchy, controls a vast part of the globe – from central Europe to the Pacific coast. From isolation in 1911, the United States has emerged from the wreckage of war as the world's leading power and, at the time of Charles's investiture, was preparing to fulfil a Wellsian dream by placing men on the moon. This venture symbolized the phenomenal degree to which science and technology had insinuated themselves into modern life, helping to foster materialism and atheism at the expense of the Christian faith.

In this particular setting the Caernarvon ceremony – indeed Britain's thousand-year-old monarchy – seems to be an anachronism, a relic of the past. Yet although Britain has lost the world's biggest empire, and her status in international affairs has diminished, the monarchy seems to be thriving. One Englishman, shrewder than most, gave the reason why. In the House of Commons Sir Winston Churchill put it thus: 'Above the ebb and flow of party strife, the rise and fall of ministries and individuals, the changes of public opinion or public fortune, the British monarchy presides, ancient, calm, and supreme within its function, over all the treasures that have been saved from the past and all the glories we write in the annals of our country.'

There is nothing to imply, even in this unpredictable age, that Prince Charles will never don the crown. But when will he do so? Strong-willed and self-assured, outwardly the Queen seems destined to live as long as the Empress Victoria. It is sometimes speculated that, unlike her great-great-grandmother, Queen Elizabeth will one day wish to abdicate in favour of her son. But this speculation ignores a vital factor. It should not be forgotten that, as Victoria exemplified in her mature years, one of the sovereign's cardinal assets, both to politicians and to the people, is the wealth of knowledge garnered during the passage of time. Prime ministers come and go but in the normal course of events the monarch reigns until death. Thus there is one central figure whose knowledge of state affairs goes unbroken over the years. The monarch is always there to be consulted by incoming ministers. Not that politicians, unfortunately, always take heed. For instance it is on record that the Queen strongly recommended her ministers not to invade Anguilla, sensibly pointing out that two frigates in the Caribbean could control the unrest then prevailing. But the government dispatched paratroopers and London policemen to subdue six thousand islanders.

Prince Charles himself does not subscribe to the notion that monarchs should be expected to retire at a specific age ('a sovereign has no pension'), emphasizing that his own contribution might be richer and more varied if it were not so bound by the constitution. One thing is certain: unlike the Prince of Wales who acceded as Edward VII in his sixtieth year, he will not be denied access to confidential matters of state. Prince Edward smarted under his mother's reluctance to inform him. When a sympathetic Gladstone arranged to furnish him with abstracts of Cabinet meetings, the Queen allowed her son to be acquainted of government decisions but insisted that a confidential report from the Prime Minister must be seen by herself alone. Prince Albert Edward wanted so desperately to be of some use to the nation, but for years the Queen declined to recognize the adroitness with which he dealt with people, his uncanny insight into character, his rare sense of diplomacy.

One cannot imagine Queen Elizabeth taking a similar myopic view. On the contrary, it is clear that the heir apparent is being groomed for kingship more subtly than any of his more recent predecessors. In this erratic, even revolutionary world, no institution – no matter how ancient its roots – can consider itself immune and invincible. A much more professional approach is imperative. The heir apparent, like the monarch, belongs to the people, and it is people and caring for their needs that matter most to the Prince. ('If people respect you, think you are worth while, then they will want you to help them with their activities, with their ventures; and if you choose to go in with them you can reasonably hope to try to influence them to do what you think is good and useful.')

10 Jack-of-all-Trades

Since those early years of the timid boy, Prince Charles has burgeoned as a young man capable of tackling situations no matter how exacting. Hence his description of himself as a Jack-of-all-Trades. Others, because of his deep-seated humour, have dubbed him the court jester from the Palace of Varieties at the end of the Mall. On a more serious note, there are those who question his unnecessary flirting with danger. For instance, it forms no part in the training for kingship – nor is it an essential part of Royal Air Force pilot training – to engage in a series of parachute jumps or go swimming beneath the Arctic ice. Neither does the role of monarch-to-be demand that Charles should participate in submarine escape training from under the sea, or pilot an aircraft to Cranwell to fulfil aerobatics in a supersonic jet. Moreover, to understand affairs of state does not require the ability to fly nuclear bombers, qualify as a commando, or, strapped in a replica of a Wessex helicopter, be dropped into a tank of water during a survival course.

Why does he confront life with what is virtually an air of bravado? Is he endeavouring to establish himself in his own right, escaping from the shadow of Prince Philip, his assertive father. When Charles was admitted as an honorary member of that charitable show-business fraternity, the Grand Order of Water Rats, he remarked: 'I always get a bit anxious when I hear that I am following in my father's footsteps. I seem to spend my life doing that. Fortunately, we wear the same size shoes.'

Perhaps, of course, he has an insatiable desire to take risks and as such is, to some extent, in the genre of the medieval warrior princes. On visiting the Virgin Island, for instance, he wrote zestfully of his reaction after diving down to a 'wreck of 1867 and experiencing the extraordinary sensation of some vast green cathedral filled with shoals of silver fish'. His enthusiasm for aqualung diving was further expressed when, off Cartagena, he located in the watery depths the dark hulk of a seventeenth-century Spanish wreck and discovered two silver pieces of eight.

Maybe it is simply a question that at heart Prince Charles is a royal adventurer who intends to savour life to the maximum as heir apparent while there is the chance. As King Charles III such antics as walking fly-like beneath the rock-hard polar ice at Resolute Bay will be strictly forbidden. Unable to stifle his sense of fun, in the tent that covered the hole broken out of the ice, he inflated his orange diving suit to surprise the photographers waiting near by. Charles later recalled: 'The result was astonishing and I looked exactly like Mr Michelin.'

One thing is certain: his courage is never in doubt. He claims that it is always 'worth challenging yourself and this is what I do most of the time. Perhaps to too great an extent sometimes – perhaps I push myself too much. But this is my outlook on life. If you're living dangerously, it tends to make you appreciate life that much more and to really want to live it to its fullest.'

Dr Bernard Camber, a psychiatrist, is on record as believing that Prince Charles visualizes himself as a warrior. But, as he comments, warriors are expendable: trained from infancy to be the future monarch, Charles is not. Many will agree that Queen Elizabeth's heir – whether or not he is seeking self-aggrandizement or focusing attention on the royal family – has no right to endanger himself. The royal family is not in need of that spectacular brand of publicity and Dr Camber doubtless attracts support in his claim that what the nation wants is a wise King, someone who cares for the people. ('He has always admired his father and at the moment he is in the same position as his father in that he has no real function or job in life. After all, the only man who made a success of being a politically powerful consort was Prince Albert. Another way of looking at it is that Charles still thinks he's in show business. But things are a bit too serious at the moment for the majority of people to show much sense of humour.')

That arch-critic of royalty, Willie Hamilton, MP, is far more forthright, contending that Prince Charles 'behaves like this to fill in the time. It is a family problem – what the Prince of Wales can do while waiting to come to the throne. Like the late Duke of Windsor, he is engaged in public relations all the time. He is projecting an image. I don't think he is exposing himself to much danger. And he is keeping himself out of the kind of trouble that Edward VIII got into. You know he would be running greater risks if he were to spend a couple of years down a coal mine ... and he would also get to know the people he is going to govern.'

The privileges of his status afford him the scope to indulge his desire 'to try all sorts of things. I do not like sitting and watching someone else doing something. I do not like going to race meetings to watch horses thundering up and down ... I would rather be riding the horses myself.' The choice of engagements during his official visit to Canada somewhat crystallized that keenness to live life to the full. In wolverine-trimmed parka ('I hope we don't meet a polar bear, it might think I'm in season'), he was shown how to build an igloo ('in case the heating fails at home'). He descended a 3,500-foot gold mine at Yellowknife and visited a natural gas field ('replenishing my jokes').

If one discards the humour and the exaggerated publicity given by the media to the more spectacular side of his life, one appreciates that basically his motive is to broaden his knowledge of men and affairs for the time that he assumes the duties of kingship. In the process he endears himself to all classes of society by his humour and charm. Typical was the underground incident at Welbeck Colliery when a miner embarrassedly explained why he spoke with difficulty. His false teeth, he said, falling on to a conveyer belt, had been carried off before he could snatch them away. 'I thought I passed a grin coming in,' replied the Prince with a reassuring smile.

The wit and the appealing personality can be applied to reap handsome dividends, too. For example, the merriment and the sambas on his South American tour rather belied the true significance of his visit. Subsequently it was announced that after descending a Venezuelan gold mine, a British firm received a £1¼ million export order to modify a gold ore treatment plant. Soon afterwards it was reported that a group of British businessmen had considered offering Prince Charles a salary of £50,000 plus attractive perquisites to represent them in the export field. The prospects of a member of the royal family responding to such overtures was absurd from the outset. The royal family cannot be partisan. Moreover, their foreign tours are never specifically in the form of trade visits, although trade and the improvement of relations need not be omitted from discussions. But the impact is there. 'There was a considerable improvement in British exports,' revealed an official of the Confederation of British Industry, 'after Prince Charles's visit to the Ivory Coast last year.'

In South America, as wherever he travels, Charles was unable to avoid the monotonous question of marriage. 'If I get married, will I be able to samba like that again?' he feinted. This obsession by the international press to end the celibacy of the most eligible bachelor in the world is almost tantamount to paranoia. From the time of the wedding of his sister, Princess Anne, to Captain Mark Phillips the press has become fatuously preoccupied with weaving a romance around him. It was enough, for example, merely to accept an invitation to shoot on the Duke of Wellington's estate in Spain to unleash a torrent of unfounded speculation about a match with Lady Jane Wellesley, the Duke's daughter. When the hospitality was returned at Sandringham in the New Year, a crowd of some ten thousand milled around the main gates to get a glimpse of the royal family and Lady Jane. Later, while addressing members of the House of Commons Press Gallery, Charles remarked that the excessive attention devoted to his unmarried status 'was predictably to be expected. There had been that crowd of ten thousand, gathered to see a certain young lady at Sandringham. I almost felt I had better espouse myself at once. As you can see, I thought better of it.' With a significant hint, he explained that 'it becomes more difficult to potter gently through the streets'.

Since then there has been a regular mart in marital predictions. Editors have regurgitated their baseless trivia to gullible or sceptical readers, as typified by one women's magazine writer who plaintively asked: 'How soon will we be let into the secret? And who will it be?' If the same writer is correct, 'there is even a sober, bespectacled tutor in London who, as Baron d'Urdal, claims to earn £20,000 a year selling gossip tips to the French press'.

Most claims by the tattlers are ridiculous. Indeed, the gossip writers are unaware of many of the Prince's social meetings. Discreet rendezvous at some intimate's home has enabled many of the Prince's female companions to escape publicity. To confuse the press, others no doubt collaborate as decoys. Accurately or not, it has been claimed that one such young lady was Laura Jo Watkins, the daughter of an American admiral, to whom the Prince was introduced at a yacht club party in San Diego. To the casual observer the outcome was somewhat puzzling. When Walter Annenberg, the US Ambassador to Britain, gave a party three months later, Laura Jo was a guest but the Prince was absent. She was present in the House of Lords when Charles made his maiden speech, and for some days basked happily in the glare of press comment, before suddenly embarking on a 'plane homeward bound'.

Some of the Prince's closest friendships stem from childhood: among them Angela Nevill, the daughter of Lord Rupert and Lady Anne Nevill, who are reputed to be the Queen's most intimate friends; Caroline Longman, to whom the Queen is godmother; and the Hon. Amanda Knatchbull, his cousin. Even if one could assume that they were even seriously considered as future consorts, a number of the Prince's girl friends have already opted for marriage with lesser mortals.

But finding a bride will present no problems to Charles. As a man he is attractive to most women. Wherever he goes he is the cynosure of feminine attention. Typical was his visit to Canada when the *Toronto Star* described 'blue-rinsed matrons nearly pushing police escorts into glass-panelled walls, women dissolving shrieking and quivering as the popular heir touched their hands and passed by'.

Prince Charles has himself said that the ideal age for marriage is 'around thirty'. This in itself is an older age for marriage among leading royal males for some decades. His father, Prince Philip, was twenty-seven years and seven months old at the time of marriage. His grandfather, King George VI, had married at twenty-seven years and four months, his great-grandfather, King George V, at twenty-eight and one week. More recently, the Duke of Gloucester was twenty-seven and the Duke of Kent twenty-five at the time of marriage. Charles's words might have been sober comment or a mischievous remark to tease the ever-inquisitive media, as on the occasion early in 1975 when he announced a meeting with the Archbishop of Canterbury. Speculation as usual ran wild. Over-imaginative minds wrongly concluded that Charles had chosen Canterbury and not Westminster Abbey as the venue of pending nuptials. When the truth emerged, he was merely attending the enthronement of the new primate, Dr Coggan.

To be the wife of Prince Charles will not necessarily be the heaven-sent blessing that so many people visualize. Much will depend on her temperament, for she must inevitably sacrifice all freedom – a loss which the Queen Mother resisted for some two years before finally yielding to the proposals of the future King George VI.

Immediately the engagement is announced Charles's fiancée will be compelled to adhere rigidly to the royal code. Whether she does so willingly or not, she will accept the inexorable life pattern and etiquette of the royal family, the centre of which is the dominant figure of her mother-in-law, the Queen. It may be many years before she and Prince Charles arrive as the incumbents of Buckingham Palace. Meanwhile, she will be the chatelaine of Chevening.

At one juncture Chevening, which was built to a plan of Inigo Jones on earlier Tudor foundations, might not have been accepted as a royal home. When the Queen and Prince Charles first saw the old desolate mansion on a chilling autumn day in 1969, they found it dilapidated and rather repelling. The sagging roof, a shored-up wall, and creeping deterioration had shed Chevening – with its curving colonnades and graceful pavilions – of its enchantment. In the nineteenth century the main edifice had been faced with tiles held by nine-inch nails which, now badly corroded, speeded forbidding decay. The royal visitors queried the suitability of Chevening as a stately home.

Fortunately Lord Stanhope, the seventh and last holder of an earldom dating from 1718 (and the thirteenth and last Earl of Chesterfield), had bequeathed a fortune for its reconditioning. When he returned to Chevening again during Easter of 1974, Prince Charles was bewitched by the transformation. The restorers had invested the ancient mansion, where William Pitt the Younger sometimes slept on visiting his nieces, with its former splendour.

There is a trace of irony in that Chevening, after a long history, should reach its zenith as a royal home. For when the third Earl succeeded to the title in 1786, he struck the Stanhope Medal inscribed 'Stanhope the friend of Trial by Jury, Liberty of the Press, Parliamentary Reform, Annual Parliaments, Habeas Corpus, etc.' and backed the French Revolution so vehemently that he removed the coronets from Chevening's gates and gloried in the proletarian name of 'Citizen Stanhope'.

The last Earl came from a different mould. A confirmed monarchist, he referred to the 'advantage particularly for the heir to the throne to have a residence near London,' especially now that Buckingham Palace is being 'overlooked from all sides, and no longer has much privacy'. Mellow Chevening, which overlooks spacious lawns, lake and beechwoods, a rural pleasance of eighty-three rooms and more than 3,500 acres – embracing parklands, farms and hamlets – could not be more ideal for a Prince and Princess of Wales. Whoever will be the chatelaine remains unknown. Meanwhile, the Squire of Chevening is proving himself an admirable potential sovereign for the twenty-first century, if not before, wishing to identify himself with the aspirations and possible resurgence of the people. He is a king of the future with a profound concern for things of the mind and the spirit. In a simple affirmation, he asserts: 'I have this feeling of duty towards England, towards the United Kingdom, the Commonwealth, and I feel that there is a great deal I can do if I am given the chance to do it.'

Select Bibliography

Arthur, Sir George, *Seven Heirs Apparent* (1937)
Cook, E. Thornton, *Kings in the Making* (1931)
Doran, Dr, *The Book of the Princes of Wales* (1860)
Fisher, Graham and Heather, *The Crown and the King* (1971)
Fisher, Graham and Heather, *Prince Charles: The Future King* (1966)
Fletcher, I. Kyrtle, *The British Court* (1953)
Grant, I. F., *The Clan Donald* (1952)
Hutchison, Harold F., *Edward II: The Pliant King* (1971)
Joelson, Annette, *Heirs to the Throne* (1966)
Morrah, Dermot, *To be a King* (1968)
Pine, L. G., *Princes of Wales* (1970)
Rothery, Guy Cadogan, *Insignia of the Princes of Wales* (1911)
Selden, John, *Titles of Honour* (1631)
Sidney, Thomas, *Heirs Apparent* (1957)
Wakeford, Geoffrey, *The Heir Apparent* (1967)
Windsor, Duke of, *A Family Album* (1960)

Index